# THE QUESTION

*A Guide to Answering Life's Most Important Question*

## JACK WILLIAMS

ISBN 979-8-88943-078-0 (paperback)
ISBN 979-8-88943-079-7 (digital)



Christian Faith Publishing
832 Park Avenue
Meadville, PA 16335
www.christianfaithpublishing.com

Printed in the United States of America

This book is dedicated to all of the IDEALS Leadership School students past, present, and future. It is a privilege to work with you and thank you for keeping me young.

If you don't know where you're going, any road can take you there.

—Lewis Carroll, *Alice in Wonderland*

## About IDEALS Foundation, Inc.
Established 1991
501-c-3 organization

### Mission
To help young people develop their leadership and life skills.

Programs

IDEALS Leadership School—established 1993, High School Student Athletes

Student Athlete Leadership Team (SALT)—established 2011, video series for HS Student Athletes

Principles for Performance—Established 2016, Life Skills video series for Career Tech HS Students

Next Step—Established 2018, Life Skills video series for HS Students

First Step—Established 2020, Life Skills video for 9th grade students

What I Wish I'd Known about High School for 9th Grade Students—Established in 2021

What I Wish I'd Known About College for 12th Grade Students—Established in 2022

THE Question: Guide to Answering Life's Most Important Question, book by Jack Williams available 2020

Websites
www.jackwwilliams.com
www.idealsleadership.org
www.nextstepprogram.org

For more information on IDEALS and any of its programs, please contact Jack Williams at jackw@idealsleadership.org

# TESTIMONIALS

Jack Williams has written a transformative book that can only be described as thought provoking, transparent, humble, and full of common-sense advice to every person regardless of age or profession. I strongly recommend it. I only wish I had read it forty years ago!
—Brent Reid CEO, Winter Companies

I met Jack Williams in 2013. Little did I know the powerful impact he would have on me. Jack introduced me to this powerful "I Believe" exercise. Based on Jack's guidance, I created my "I Believe" list, and it changed my life. It will change your life too!
—John Vaughn, author of *The Accountability Changes Everything Journal*

Jack Williams's *The Question* book and "I Believe" list provides a wonderful roadmap for a life of integrity and purpose. Jack's life learnings in sports, business, and leadership development, serve the reader well in their pursuit of success and purpose in all phases of life.
—Vance Bell CEO, Shaw Industries

Jack Williams not only communicates the importance of the right foundation for our lives, but also he walks us through the importance of a daily commitment to it. Using his own life experiences, the book is personal, humorous, and timely.
—Tom Richardson, President, Atlanta Dental

Destiny is a choice, not a chance!
Jack Williams's *The Question* provides the
playbook to discover yours.
Cherish the journey.
—John Dewberry, CEO, Dewberry Group

Jack Williams has seen the world from the top of the mountain
and from the deepest gulley. This book reflects the importance
of beliefs and values regardless of one's station in life. Jack does
an excellent job of laying out in a very readable and enjoyable
format what is important in life and how leadership, humility, and
vision are the cornerstones of an effective life. The stories of this
book are the stories of a life well lived and the wisdom that can
come only from having walked the path. Jack Williams is a gifted
writer, and his account of what he believes serves as a blueprint
for becoming an effective citizen and a caring individual. It will
make you a better person and a better leader and will inspire
everyone, young and old, to a life of greater service. Enjoy the ride.
—Jimmy C. Stokes, EdD, Retired Executive Director,
Georgia Association of Educational Leaders

The number one skill that employers continue to state is missing
in most entry-level workers is soft/life skills. One of the most basic
fundamentals of developing strong life skills is understanding
what you believe. What are the principles you are going to use
to guide you through life? We've asked Jack to teach these skills
at workshops for Georgia Career, Technical, and Agriculture
Education (CTAE) educators. Jack has taken content from his
workshops and uses passion, humor, and real-life experiences
to address this serious subject in this impactful book.
—Dr. Barbara Wall—State Director Georgia Career,
Technical, and Agriculture Education.

Jack has written a common-sense book about a belief system
of values, morals, and principles that everyone can relate to,
and he has combined them with some of his real-life stories
and experiences. Most everyone could benefit by taking some
time to read this short book of "I Believe" statements. Most
of us know these to be true… Jack just reminded us!
—Steven W. Williams, Regional President
United Community Bank

Jack quickly gets to the heart of leadership by challenging the reader
to develop core belief statements that guide everyday life. I strongly
urge you to follow Jack's guide and get started on your list as I have.
—Chuck Warbington, City Manager,
City of Lawrenceville, Georgia

Jack has inspired me, my family, my athletic staff, and thousands
of others through his various leadership programs. He is a man
of uncommon and uncompromised priorities with a purposeful
desire to make a positive influence in the lives of others. In *The
Question*, Jack writes about establishing and integrating one's beliefs
into every aspect of their life. He reveals profound principles for
living and being an impactful role model. It is an easy read with
many practical applications and interesting stories. I'm certain it
will improve the professional and personal life of all who read it.
—Dexter Wood, Athletic Director, Buford, Georgia

# CONTENTS

# PREFACE

The book you are about to read is a simple story about one of the most meaningful exercises I went through in my life. It revolved around me asking myself a simple question: What are my core values, principles, or beliefs? The answer to that question resulted in providing a foundation to use to guide me through the various challenges and opportunities that life presents. It was a game changer in my life, and I hope it will be for you as well.

Overall, I have written content for thirty-four videos, countless workshops, and keynote talks, but I have never written a book before. I assumed it would follow the same process. And to be truthful, there definitely is some carryover; however, it has been a great learning experience as well. I kind of went about the process backward. I wrote my first rough draft without consulting anyone who had experience writing a book. This was not the smartest thing to do considering I had a brother who had written several books and who also taught workshops on the subject. You would think I would have gone to him and others that I knew who had written books *before* I started writing, but not this guy.

After I'd completed my first draft and then my first personal proofing, I got wise and decided to check with my more experienced and talented brother. So I asked him and several others to read my manuscript and give me their thoughts. I chose different people who I knew would tackle the assignment from different perspectives with varying degrees of detail. All of these folks really helped, and they did, in fact, approach the assignment as I had predicted. My brother really helped me and shared some great advice. Simple but great, and that is why it was great. I can follow simple! He asked me several questions, but the two most important ones were: *What is the purpose of the book? What do I want the reader to get out of it?*

As I mentioned, the advice was simple and straightforward. One might say, it's also just good common sense. Well, it might be, but this old boy must be lacking in that category because I hadn't asked myself those two direct questions. These questions also forced me to more specifically consider who my audience was going to be. You see, I was so excited to actually get my thoughts on paper, that I just started writing, following the same process as when I speak or conduct a leadership or life skills workshop, but there was a difference. When I would do a workshop, I would tailor the content to that specific audience. I had to in order for it to be impactful.

When I first started writing this book, in my misguided vision of being the next *New York Times* best-selling author, I was thinking all audiences were going to be my audience. And to my defense, any audience could benefit from the book. However, I decided to shape the examples and stories to be geared to the adult reader. I decided I could write a second edition for youth.

Now let's go back to the two questions above.

*What is the purpose of the book?*

I spent a lot of time writing down a lot of verbiage in answering the question and later realized I needed to be more succinct in my answer. I boiled down the answer to this.

Life is not easy. It comes at us from all angles and requires us to have a firm foundation to handle the challenges it brings. It is critical for people to understand the benefit of putting their values, beliefs, principles, etc., in writing and to use that to help guide them through their lives.

*What do I want the reader to get out of the book?*

I want the readers to develop a well-thought-out list of belief statements and understand the importance of having the discipline and commitment to review that list on a regular basis. As they do,

I would like them to allow it to guide them to live their lives based on what they truly believe and not to be influenced by the outside world, which will constantly be challenging many of those beliefs.

In the book, I break down my *I Believe* statements into the following categories:

- Decisions
- Relationships
- Character
- Communication
- Attitude
- Family
- Money
- Faith

Having spent four years playing college football and then coaching college football for another seven years, I have included some sports stories in the book to demonstrate some of my key points. For those of you who are not big sports fans, don't worry there are plenty of stories and examples you'll be able to easily relate to.

Also, I tried to be completely transparent in my personal examples. Some of those stories and examples were difficult to share and, quite frankly, were somewhat embarrassing to put in print. That said, when I share this message to live audiences, I share these same stories.

After each *I Believe* statement, you'll be given a couple action items to consider for your personal application of the statement. I've left space in the book for you to put your answers for easy reference in the future. At the end of each chapter, you'll see a space for what I call "takeaways." This space is for you to write down any general thoughts you want to "takeaway" from the content shared in that chapter. I want to really encourage you to use this space to summarize your thoughts. Don't just turn the page to the next chapter.

Another goal of this book was to make it meaningful, easy to read, interactive, and humorous, and to create what I call "stickiness" with the reader. By "stickiness," I'm referring to the reader integrating what he or she learned through creating a personal *I Believe* list, with the hopes of it making a difference in their lives, just as this experience has made in mine.

I hope you enjoy your time in the book, but more importantly, I hope you will be encouraged to immediately start working on your personal *I Believe* list!

# INTRODUCTION

There is a framed quote from Robert Byrne above the credenza in my office that reads, "*The purpose of life is a life of purpose.*" He captured a simple but powerful formula for a meaningful life.

I think it's fair to say that the majority of people would like to say they have had a meaningful life. Meaningful could mean different things to different people, but let's define it as the following: a life that had purpose, was fulfilling, and made you feel like you made a difference in some way. In order to have that meaningful life, there needs to be a blueprint to follow that can guide you through the steps to accomplish that goal. Blueprints are crucial to achieving anything worthwhile. Life can be tough, and even blueprints have to be modified sometimes because someone once said, "*Life is what happens while we are making other plans.*" We have to make adjustments, but in order to make adjustments, you first have to have a plan or blueprint.

Okay, a blueprint is important, but I want to share what I think is equally important—knowing who you are and what you believe in.

I'm convinced that if I went into any area of the country and stuck a microphone in front of people and asked them to write down ten things that are core beliefs, most of the people would hesitate because they really hadn't thought about that question.

They've thought about

- what college they wanted to attend,
- the type of person they would like to marry,
- what type of career they wanted to pursue,
- where they would like to live,
- who their favorite actors/actresses are,

- where should they invest their money, and
- what their favorite restaurants are.

There is nothing wrong with any of these areas, but what about these simple, yet very profound questions?

- Who are you?
- What are your core values?
- What are the principles that you want to guide you through life?

Those were questions I asked myself in 1993. That's the good news. The bad news is I was forty-four years old when I got around to asking those questions. I wished I had asked those questions when I was much younger in life because it would have surely saved me a lot of frustration, embarrassment, pain, wasted time, and effort. That said, I was grateful that at least, I got around to it at forty-four. Fortunately, I've been blessed many years after that age to benefit from addressing those key questions.

I don't know what age bracket you fall in. Regardless of what it is, the answers to these questions have great value and meaning in a person's life at any and every age.

I decided to wrap these three questions into one simple but challenging exercise. I decided to put in writing sentences that begin with the two words *I* Believe. Here is my story. I hope it can soon be your story as well.

# CHAPTER 1

# My Story

The privilege of a lifetime is being who you are.
—Joseph Campbell

It was 1993, and I was out jogging and listening to a tape. For those of you under the age of forty, you might need to google *cassette tape*. The subject on the tape dealt with the concept of principles and how important it was for a person to understand the value of living a principle-centered life. Well, I knew what a principle was; however, when I got back home, I looked it up in the dictionary for a more detailed definition. Again, for those of you under forty, we didn't have *Dictionary.com*. People actually had to go to a hard copy book to look up words. To make the meaning relevant in today's world, I have listed definitions you would find if you looked it up in *Dictionary.com* today. This is what I found:

- An accepted or professed rule of action or conduct
- A fundamental, primary or general law or truth from which others are derived
- A fundamental doctrine or tenet; a distinctive opinion
- A personal or specific basis of conduct
- Guiding sense of the requirements and obligations of right conduct
- An adopted rule or method for application in action

When I completed my search in 1993, I decided to condense the various definitions in the dictionary to come up with my personal definition. I believe a principle is really represented by your values and beliefs. I realized like most of us, I'd never really taken the time to put down in writing what "I believed." We all know writing something down creates more awareness and "stickiness" in terms of retention and meaning. Therefore, I began my exercise by simply getting a legal pad and a pen and started writing down statements that began with the two words, *I believe*. Let me stop here for a minute. When you start writing a sentence in ink that begins with the two words, *I believe*, you better think carefully about what you write down. I began writing down whatever came to mind, and the statements were not in any order or priority. Later, as I began to teach a class on creating your *I Believe* list to young people and adults, I recommended that they come up with a list of areas in their lives that might warrant an *I Believe* statement. This exercise would have made my thought process a little more organized, had I done it when writing my original *I Believe* list. We'll come back to this later.

I carried my "work-in-progress" list with me when I traveled and kept adding *I Believe* statements when one came to mind. The process lasted several weeks, and I finally felt like I had a pretty comprehensive list. My original list contained sixty-nine personal *I Believe* statements that related to all aspects of my life.

Now I thought that was going to be the hard part of the process, but little did I know that was just the beginning. I realized that if I didn't keep this list in the front of my mind, it was going to later result in just a lengthy exercise that had no long-term value. I could convince myself it was a worthwhile effort just to go through the process, but if it didn't result in some positive behavior change on my part, was it really worth the effort? It's like going to hear a motivational speaker and you're so pumped when you leave. However, after a few days, your actions fall back to your original behavior patterns prior to hearing the speaker. Your intentions were good, but your follow through was lacking. The only person who truly benefitted from that experience was the motivational speaker when he cashed the check! I didn't want that type of experience to happen with my *I Believe* list.

Here's what I decided to do. I want to repeat what I said earlier. The decision to create my personal "I Believe" list and then to follow the plan I'm about to share with you has been a real game changer in my life.

Okay, let's get started.

Step 1 is the step mentioned earlier that I didn't use when I wrote my original *I Believe* list. It would have really helped me to organize my thoughts and would have given some order to the process had I done so. Now when I teach a class on my *I Believe* list, I include this as the first step for those who hopefully will create their personal list. The first step is to create a list of areas in one's life that one might want to consider creating an *I Believe* statement about. Some examples are money, finances, relationships, family, etc.

Step 2 is for you to actually start your list. Don't worry about having the perfect wording for each statement; the key thing is to get the main point of the statement in writing. You'll do what I did and continue to play with the statements later until you get them the way you want them to read.

Now comes Step 3. It will be your biggest challenge, but it's the *key* to this whole activity. Step 3 is to read your *I Believe* list *every* morning, Monday through Friday, *each* week. Not most mornings or some mornings or when you are home or have time, read it every morning, read it before you start your day. No exceptions.

For the first eleven years, I read my list *each* morning, Monday through Friday. I didn't miss a day. Maybe I should have extended it to Saturday and Sunday, but I wanted to read it before I started my workday. After eleven years, I switched to reading the list each Monday morning to start my week. I'm happy to say as of the writing of this book in 2020, I haven't missed a week!

Okay, I said it was a game changer. Let me explain why. First, just the self-discipline of starting your day off by reinforcing what you believe in is really positive. I don't know about you, but most of my days consisted of having things pop up that required me to make decisions regarding how to handle or react to something. Reading what I said I believed in on those mornings, kept it fresh on my mind and helped me work through the appropriate response. I'm not going to say I didn't screw up some of those situations and sometimes contradicted what was on my list, but those exceptions became fewer and fewer as the number of repetitions increased.

The other thing that the consistent reading of my *I Believe* list did was serve as an accountability tool. I'd be reading my list, and all of a sudden, I'd have a flashback to something the day before where my behavior didn't support my specific *I Believe* statement. This process will be a work in progress. You're not going to be able to 100 percent match your behavior to reflect everything on your list. Well, at least I haven't been able to do it yet and may never, but what it will do is keep you focused on these key beliefs, and your behavior will become more in alignment with your beliefs as you continue to work the process. But I guarantee you, I'm batting a much higher percentage than had I not created the list and read it daily.

Here's what I did and still do when I have a situation where my behavior doesn't match what was in my statement: I put an asterisk by that statement in pencil to remind me I have work to do. There can be several reasons for that happening, but it doesn't matter. Don't beat yourself up over it. Acknowledge the reality of the situation, asterisk it, and focus on removing that asterisk in the near future.

I'd love to tell you that every single asterisk on my personal *I Believe* list has been removed, but that wouldn't be true. Here's where the true reality check comes into play, the part that tests if you really are serious about your list. If after a period of time—and you have to determine what that particular period is—your behavior hasn't changed to the point where your actions are in support of your statement, then you have to remove that statement from your list.

If you think writing your *I Believe* statements in ink is hard, think about what it feels like when you have to admit your behavior doesn't support keeping it on your list and you have to strike through it. I can tell you I know exactly how that feels, and it's not a feeling I recommend. That said, if you really do a thorough job in creating your list, my guess is, you'll probably be faced with doing just that sometime in the future. Remember, I said this is a work in progress. You can always add the statement back at a future date if you're willing to make the necessary changes to your behavior. Again, don't beat yourself up over it.

Step 4 in this process is to continue to update your *I Believe* list with new statements that you feel should be added. I'm currently on the tenth edition of my list. I've taken some off that I couldn't support through my behavior, and I've also replaced some that just didn't seem as important as when I wrote them. Some statements were too generic and not personal enough, so I revised them or replaced them with a more accountable version. I will also add that after I wore out the first few handwritten copies, I put my list on the computer to make it easier to work with.

At the back of the book, you'll find a list of potential areas of one's life that might serve as a guide in developing your list. It is now called step 1 of the process. I mentioned that I didn't do this the first time when I created my list, but I did go back and create this list later as a follow up to review. You'll also find a copy of the tenth edition (current copy) of my personal *I Believe* list.

Well, I've just broken every rule in the book regarding writing a book. In the first few pages, I've shared what the book is about, why I wrote it, how to do what I recommend, and how to make it work for you. You have everything you need to get started, but as they say in those infomercials, there's more!

In the next part of the book, I'm going to share some of my statements and why I think they are important. When I present the talk on my *I Believe* list live, I go through many of the items on my list as potential teaching points for those in the audience. I'm confident those who have attended my sessions would *strongly* encourage you to read on because of the value they received as I went into some detail and background behind some of my statements. The reason I say teaching points is that I think you might relate to many of the items and reasoning behind putting them down. There are also others you may have never even considered creating a statement for on your list. Some you'll just get a kick out of.

One of the statements on my list is *I Believe* in always continuing to learn and improve. I hope that's what you'll do and stay with me as I share some of my statements with you. It's your call, but I hope you'll join me.

# CHAPTER 2

## *I Believe* Statements

If you don't stand for something, you'll fall for anything.
—Alexander Hamilton

All right! You're still with me. Thanks for resisting the temptation to take the "secret sauce" and start doing your own thing. In this section, I am going to take my *I Believe* list and break the statements into the various areas of life that they are associated with. Several of my statements could be placed in multiple categories, but for our discussion, we'll just leave them in one category.

Let me make a very important point here before we go any further. This is *my* list. I'm going to share things that Jack Williams believes in. I'm in no way saying my beliefs need to be your beliefs. You may agree with some of my beliefs and disagree with others. That's fine. Each individual has to make those personal decisions about the principles, beliefs, and truths that are going to guide his or her life. The purpose of sharing my list is to let you see the various types of statements that make up my list and hopefully encourage and motivate you to create your own.

My *I Believe* list began by attempting to create something that would be a foundational list of beliefs that would guide me personally, spiritually, and in the relationships in my life. Many of the statements apply equally to business as well. At a later time, I started my *Business and Leadership I Believe* lists, but we won't get into any items from that list in this book. However, as previously stated, many statements off my personal list could apply equally well in a business or leadership scenario.

As I was writing this book, I had no idea what the demographics of the readers, particularly in reference to age, would look like. I've tried to make my comments such that multiple age groups would be able to relate, but there are probably some suggestions or comments that might relate more to one age group or another.

After each statement and my comments associated with it, you'll find space titled—*Personal Application*. This space is there for you to think about how that statement might apply to your life and if so, to respond in writing to the question asked. Use the space for any thoughts or comments you are inclined to write. My hope is that many of these statements will inspire you to take an objective look at your life and generate some thoughts or action items to think about. They may trigger a similar statement that you might want to use on your *I Believe* list. This is the place where you can record your thoughts and ideas.

Before I get into my list and you start completing the *Personal Application* sections, I need to place each of you under oath.

Raise your right hand and repeat after me: "I solemnly swear to tell the truth, the whole truth, and nothing but the truth; so help me God."

If you aren't honest in your assessments and questions shared in the *Personal Application* section, you're missing a great opportunity to make some positive changes in your life. As you read through some of my personal stories that relate directly to some of my *I Believe* statements, you'll notice that I'm very transparent with you and I don't even know you. All I ask is you be perfectly transparent with someone you know intimately—yourself!

For simplicity's sake, I've broken down my statements into eight categories. As mentioned earlier, when you begin your personal *I Believe* exercise, you'll want to come up with a more exhaustive list of categories or areas of your life that you feel might warrant an *I Believe* statement. Remember there is an example of this that can be found at the end of the book. For the book, I'm not breaking the categories into that type of detail. Also, I'm not going to provide a narrative for all of the statements on my list; however, I've selected a number of them to share. Again, the complete list can be found at the back of the book.

I have chosen to share some selected statements off my *I Believe* list from the following categories:

- Decisions
- Relationships
- Character
- Communication
- Attitude
- Family
- Money
- Faith

These categories are not listed in any order of priority or importance. Also, the statements shown in each category are not in any order related to priority.

Now let's dive right into these statements.

# CHAPTER 3

# Decisions

There are three constants in life…change, choice, and principle.
—Stephen Covey

*I Believe we all make decisions, and ultimately our decisions will make us.*

I have to first come clean on this one. This statement was actually taken from a car commercial that Tiger Woods was doing during the height of his success as a golfer. I don't recall if this was the exact wording he used, but it was close, and I thought it made a great point. The message conveyed in the commercial was that Tiger made the decision to sacrifice and do things others wouldn't do (decision), and as a result of that decision, he became one of the greatest golfers of all time. The car company wanted the audience to think that by purchasing their luxury car, it would make a statement of who they are and the status they had attained.

I want to share a personal story in which this statement really hit home.

I was serving as a regional vice president in a $700 million service company that rented work uniforms to our customer base. Without any hint of a change coming, our CEO called me in and told me I was being promoted to senior vice president/division general manager of our $220 million uniform division. I was obviously thrilled about the opportunity. That excitement quickly subsided a couple of days later when that same CEO brought in all three division general managers to tell us we needed an immediate 3 percent price increase because our sales number was below where it needed to be at that time of the year.

Nothing wrong about a leader reacting to a sales shortfall, but in this case, it became a credibility issue with me. You see, our company's contract with our customers allowed us to have one price increase a year, and as a company, we had implemented that increase in all three divisions a few months prior. Now the CEO was asking us to do it again, even though our contract didn't allow it.

I understood the pressure my boss was under; we were not tracking to hit our sales number for the year. I knew the company needed to increase our sales in order to hit that sales goal. In a publicly traded company, hitting sales and profit goals are extremely important. Shareholders are watching those numbers very closely and react negatively when they are trending in the wrong direction. I just didn't agree with the solution my boss had chosen.

I had scheduled a national meeting with my three regional vice presidents and all of their plant general managers to go over my plans for the division that upcoming weekend, and now this bombshell gets dropped on me. I quickly realized how I responded to this issue could easily define my leadership "brand" with our division. I decided to go meet with our CEO and share that I had a problem with the price increase and explained why. It was a short meeting. I told him I couldn't do the price increase, but I would figure a way to get the 3 percent increase in sales for our division. His encouraging words were something like, *"It would be in your best interest to do so."*

I immediately called our three regional vice presidents together and explained the situation and let them know that the agenda for our weekend meeting had changed. Our number 1 priority was to figure out how to get the uptick in sales without violating the terms of our contract. They agreed, as did our CFO. I opened up our meeting by welcoming the group and letting them know I considered it a privilege to be working with them. I then held up the original agenda for the meeting and tore it in half. I explained our weekend agenda had now dramatically changed. I clarified why I balked on the price increase because I believed the group felt the same way I did about the integrity of our contract and long-term relationships with our customers.

Violating a contract is usually the beginning of the end of a relationship, and none of us wanted that to happen. I told them we were going to break out into our three Regions and each Region was going to be tasked with coming up with some creative, yet legitimate ways to create a 3 percent increase in our sales base.

After spending that night and part of Saturday working on ideas, each group presented their thoughts, and we focused our efforts on a couple of the initiatives recommended. The most significant recommendation focused on adding an environmental charge to each invoice based on the fact that oil prices had increased dramatically, and we had not passed any of that cost on to our customers. We were able to do this without affecting their price for the individual uniform rental, which was directly tied to our contract.

We also decided to address an issue that had been causing us serious problems for a while, and we just hadn't decided what to do about it. Some of our customers were abusing our garments, resulting in the garments wearing out prematurely and our company having to replace them. This was an added cost that wasn't factored into our pricing when we originally signed the contract with our customer. It wasn't a widespread issue, but it was significant enough to address with those customers where it applied, and now was going to be a great time and opportunity to do so.

Neither of these actions, the environmental charge, and the abused garment charge was prohibited by our contract, and they were, in fact, justifiable charges. They actually should have been implemented before this time. We were able to reach our 3 percent goal, while our other two divisions were dealing with significant customer complaints and were suffering customer defections negating the price increase they chose to implement.

What could have been a disaster for my first week on the job turned out to be a great opportunity for our leadership team to make a statement about how we were going to conduct our business. It was a great platform to show that values, principles, and contracts matter.

Fortunately for me, I had just recently gone through the exercise of creating my personal *I Believe* list. I'm convinced it played a major role in helping me make the decision about the direction our division was going to take on this issue. I'd like to believe that I would have handled the situation in a similar manner had I not gone through this. That said, to be totally transparent, it would have really been tempting to "lean" toward not rocking the boat with our CEO after I'd just been promoted and implement the price increase to see what would have happened.

*What are some decisions that you are facing now that relate to your principles, values, and beliefs?*

## Personal Application

---

*I Believe there are always going to be consequences to our decisions—good or bad.*

This statement aligns with the previous one. They go hand in hand. The fact is all of our lives are going to be a reflection of the decisions that we make, both good and bad, and those reflections are going to say a great deal about who we are.

Too often, people will not think through the consequences associated with making a poor decision. If it's a decision that is minor in nature, the consequences may be relatively insignificant. On the other hand, certain decisions will definitely play a major role in shaping who we are, who we become, and the life we live, as a result of those decisions.

Let's take a minute and look at two questions that affect decision-making.

- What are some factors that can affect decision-making?
- Why can good people still make bad decisions?

Let's start with some of the factors that can influence decision-making. If you think through this question, I am sure you can come up with quite a comprehensive list. However, for our purposes in this book, I'm going to share just some key variables.

- Belief system—values, morals, principles (you could say our *I Believe* list)
- Options—How many choices are available?
- Facts/perceptions—What are the facts about the situation, or do I even have enough facts to make a decision? Are they facts or perceptions? Perceptions are okay, as long as you realize they are perceptions and may not be facts.
- Time—How much time do I have? Am I being rushed?
- Risk—What are the potential consequences if I make the wrong decision? What if I don't make a decision at all?
- Family—How could this affect my family? Have I discussed it with them? Why not?
- Friends—Are they trying to get involved? What is their motive for doing so?
- Money—Can I financially afford this decision?
- Ego—Is ego becoming a factor in this process?
- Emotions—Am I clearly thinking through this decision, or are my emotions coming into play?

Any of these or a combination of these factors can affect a person's decision-making process.

I know what you're thinking. You're thinking, *"I'm a pretty sharp person. I know how to make good decisions."*

That may well be the case, but let's explore how good, sharp people like you can still make bad decisions.

Here are a few reasons how that can happen:

- They get rushed or waited to the last minute, and now time is working against them instead of for them.
- They are uninformed.
- They become impatient and rush the process.
- They don't have all the facts.
- They didn't think it through.
- They were influenced by others.
- Maybe they really don't care.
- They could be selfish.
- They are reacting instead of thinking.
- They let their ego make the decision for them.
- They didn't ask for advice or help.

There are obviously other reasons that can come into play, but the point I want to make about decision-making is that it is not a simple process and shouldn't be treated as such.

Okay, we've established maybe decision-making is not as easy as it seems sometimes. What about the potential consequences? Our statement says there will always be consequences to all of our decisions, either good or bad. That is a true statement. As I mentioned earlier, some consequences may be insignificant because the decision was a minor one. Other times, the consequences could be life changing. Think about some of these types of decisions—lifestyle choices, marriage, education, finances, career, home, retirement, etc. We need to be aware of the potential consequences on the front end before we make the decisions. We need not only to be mindful of the consequences as it relates to us but also how it could affect others around us.

I want to share a story about a young man I was recruiting when I was an assistant football coach at Georgia Tech. The story is well documented, so I'm not sharing anything confidential. Even though this information is public knowledge, I'm still going to use a different name for the individual involved to tell my story. Let's refer to him as Bill. He played high school football in Virginia in the early 1970s. He was an extremely sharp young man with solid grades, great athletic talent, and a personality that everyone wanted to be around. He also exhibited strong leadership potential.

Bill and I hit it off right away, and back then, coaches could have unlimited contact with the recruits. I was obviously spending a lot of time in Virginia, for he was the top prospect I was recruiting that year by far. Bill was so talented that he was being recruited by many of the proverbial "schools across the country." He would be classified in today's terms as a "five-star recruit."

I was visiting Bill one day and the usual type of conversation was occurring; however, all of a sudden, it changed. Bill asked me one simple question.

He said, "Coach, it's $8,000. Are you in or are you out?"

Well, I can assure you I wasn't ready for that type of question because nothing in our relationship or Bill's background indicated we might go down this path. For those of you unfamiliar with recruiting, schools are not supposed to pay players to attend their school. This was prior to the name, image, and likeness compensation college athletes can legally receive. That is what we call *cheating*. I was trying to buy some time and gather my thoughts, so I played dumb, which is a role I'm well qualified to play.

I responded, "Bill, what does $8,000 get me?"

Bill quickly replied, "It puts you in the quarter-finals to keep recruiting me."

Well, I knew it was time to pack my bags, check out of the hotel, turn in my rental car, and return to Atlanta. We were no longer going to be recruiting Bill. Before I left, I thought this might be a good time for a teaching moment for good ole Bill.

I said, "Bill, let me share a thought with you. Because you had made some good decisions in your life up to this point, you had placed yourself on this interstate highway that would take you wherever you wanted to go. But just a minute ago, you told me you were going to turn on your blinker and take an exit ramp. Bill, if you take that exit ramp, I can assure you, you'll never get back on that interstate again."

I have to stop here and say I was feeling pretty good about myself. With no notice to prepare, I was able to come up with a great analogy that I thought ought to really make him think.

While I'm patting myself on the back, Bill said, "I guess that means you're out." So much for my *"Attaboy"* Coach Jack.

I said, "Bill, you are correct. Good luck."

Well, let's see how this decision-making exercise ended up. Bill ended up signing with a major college university, which at that time had been subject to allegations of paying some players to come to their school. That said, I guess it was a good "investment" for the school because Bill was *Conference Defensive Player of the Year* his senior year and was a first-round NFL draft pick.

Flash forward a few years later, Bill played six years in the NFL and never became a real star. He then bounced around a few years in another new football league that came into existence back then. The finale of Bill's story came in October 1987 when I read in the *Atlanta Journal* that Bill had tragically taken his own life. He had allegedly been a suspect in two convenience store robberies prior to his death.

Now when someone takes his own life, there are usually a lot of things happening at that time. I have no idea what was occurring in Bill's life when he made that decision. What I do know is this: Here was a guy who had a great future ahead but unfortunately became a good guy who made a series of bad decisions, resulting in a terrible, tragic ending. Yes, there are consequences to our decisions.

*What can you start doing differently to improve your decision-making process?*

At the end of this section on decisions, I'm going to share some recommendations on how you could do just that.

## Personal Application

---

*I Believe in doing just the next right thing.*

My comments here will be shorter than the last two. I'm a positive person (except for my issue regarding a tendency to be judgmental, which you'll hear about later). I think most people know the difference between right and wrong, and for the most part, want to do the right thing. There are obviously exceptions out there that cause problems for all of us, but let's assume the majority of people don't fall into that category.

One simple rule that I've found to be helpful when trying to make a decision or work toward some long-term goal, is to ask a straightforward question. That question is, "What is the next right thing to do?"

Making a decision is sometimes a process that requires multiple steps in order for it to be successful. It's not a one-step deal. By choosing to do "just the next right thing," it simplifies your choices and reduces the likelihood of a major consequence. If you keep asking yourself this question along the way, your path will become clearer and more straightforward. It will eliminate a lot of the "noise" that can come into play when trying to make a decision. This really comes into play as you work your way toward a possible long-term goal that might seem unattainable right now.

Using the concept of doing "just the next right thing" doesn't just apply to goals you're working toward; it applies to anytime you have to make a decision.

I'm going to stop my commentary right here and turn the authorship over to you to complete this section. I want you to think about a decision or goal that you're working on right now. It could be any area of your life: relationships, finances, work, school, community, etc.

*In the Personal Application section, I want you to write down what those issues are and then ask your self—"What is the next right thing I should do in each one of them?"*

## Personal Application

---

*I Believe in seeking wise counsel on important issues. I don't have all the answers.*

Boy, I wish I'd understood this truth far sooner than I did. I think back to some of the stupid decisions I made because I didn't seek out other people's advice. Not asking for guidance or input is a common practice. It seems like seeking help from others would just be the common-sense thing to do. If that's the case, why don't we do it?

I'll give you my opinion. We've developed, if you want to use that term in this analogy, as a society to where asking someone for help is seen as a sign of weakness. I personally think it's just the opposite. In fact, I think it shows a sign of maturity. An individual is demonstrating humility and transparency by saying, "I don't know everything. I still have a lot to learn, and I'd really like your help."

Most people really like to help others. It's an inherent trait when asked to help to do so. Think about how you feel when someone comes to you and asks for your advice or input on something. The first reaction should be humility because the person thinks enough of you to ask you to get involved. Most people are very open to help-ing someone when asked.

The other part of this equation is we don't know everything. We *do* need help. We just have to get over the mindset that it's a sign of weakness to reach out to someone who you think can add value to a situation you're dealing with.

Let me share a simple example of realizing you don't know everything and need to ask for help.

I grew up in a family where my father was good at working with his hands. However, that wasn't his occupation. He was in sales, but he loved working around the house and yard and building things. He had a good mechanical mind and loved tools. Unfortunately, we've all heard about generations skipping traits. Well, this particular trait of my father got a running start and pole-vaulted right over me.

While coaching in Virginia, I had purchased a house that had loosely laid bricks in the form of a U-shaped driveway. The original owner had laid them but never bonded them together. The u-drive also had a straight extension leading up to the side entrance to the house. It was a good idea that never got finished and looked a little odd to me. When I looked at the drive, I didn't see loosely laid bricks. In my mind, I could envision these bricks being moved and trans-formed into a brick patio and BBQ grill in my backyard. My dad had put a brick BBQ grill in our back yard, and I wanted one too.

I read up on how to lay bricks, and it didn't seem like it would be too hard of a thing to do, so I went ahead and started seriously researching how to do it. I was honest with myself and knew I was going to have to pay someone to do the grill. That, I knew, was going to be higher than my pay grade, but laying bricks, I can do that.

One afternoon, I was bragging to one of my neighbors about my patio plans.

He said, "Make sure you don't do what Bobby did and build it over your septic tank."

We both laughed, and I said, "This may be a new project for me, but I wouldn't do something stupid like that."

I immediately ran in and called my real estate agent to ask where the septic tank was located because I had no idea! He told me, and I exhaled a sigh of relief because it wasn't in the area I had planned for the patio and grill.

It now was time to do my handiwork. I had a week's vacation coming up from my coaching job, and patio-making was on the agenda. I had done the research and was ready to display my craftsmanship. I first dug out the area that I had envisioned was the best place for the patio. I dug it to the depth the books said to and then painfully leveled and leveled and then leveled some more to make sure the area where the bricks were to be placed was perfectly flat. Day 1 was completed, and I was feeling pretty good.

I got upstairs, showered, and was mentally patting myself on the back when my real estate agent called and asked if I had started my project. I proudly explained all that I had accomplished that day. I then asked why he called.

He said, "I made a mistake when I told you where your septic tank was." My heart sank. I was thinking, *Please don't tell me what I think you're about to tell me.* Yep. My tank was located directly under part of my perfectly dug out patio area.

After trying to not show any emotion or *hatred* toward my agent, I hung up the phone and flopped down on the bed totally distraught. Then the competitor in me, the craftsman in me arose, and I thought, *I dug the first area. I can redesign and still get this project completed. It will just have a slightly different look.*

After thinking about how to redesign it so it wouldn't cover the septic tank, I realized this new design actually looked pretty good. I went out the next day and made the changes I needed to make and leveled the entire area again. My real estate agent didn't call. It was a good day. Day 2 complete.

On day 3, the laying of the bricks began. For you "wannabe" bricklayers, when laying brick, you have to first pick the pattern you want for the space. I'd looked at several patterns and had made my choice. I began laying the bricks and then filling in between the brick with the sandy cement that was going to bond the bricks together.

Laying brick is a tedious, slow-moving process because you have to keep making sure everything stays level and the pattern doesn't begin to "move" in the process. Days 3 and 4 totally consisted of laying bricks. As I was into day 4, I realized my pattern was slightly off. It actually had started the latter part of day 3, and I was so focused on getting the remaining bricks down that I forgot to keep monitoring the pattern. Now I was beginning to panic a little. I had one more day to get this project completed. I had already made other plans for the weekend. So I went back and tried my best to get the pattern back aligned. It was "reasonably close," and then I worked to get the remaining bricks in place.

As evening fell in Charlottesville, Virginia, that Friday, I still had some bricks that had not been put into place, and I was totally exhausted. I rationalized in my mind that I was bringing in a brick mason to build the BBQ, so I'll just ask him to finish the last part of the patio before he starts on the grill. No big deal and shouldn't cost that much for him to put the finishing touches on my masterful project.

I went to bed that evening thinking my dad would really be proud of me. Even though I hadn't quite completed the project, I'd done well!

On Monday, Coach Williams went back to coaching and the brick mason came to do his work. I got home Monday night and immediately went to the back yard to see what progress the brick mason had made. To my amazement, I saw he had totally completed the work on the patio and the BBQ grill and did it in one day. I was impressed. The patio looked even better than I thought it would.

I went upstairs and told my wife what a great idea I had to use those old bricks and how good I felt about building my own brick patio. I also mentioned I was a little surprised that the brick mason was able to do the work in one day.

My wife grinned and said, "Yeah, it was, particularly considering he picked up every brick you had laid and started over on the patio. He said he didn't want his name associated with a patio that looked the way yours did!"

Lesson learned. I didn't know everything. For sure, I didn't know all there was to build a brick patio. When I did ask for help and went to the right person for that help, a far better project was completed.

Before we leave this subject, I want to mention one other point. I alluded to this in the sentence above. I went to the *right* person for help, and that is crucial. I realized later in business to not just pick out someone who might be available. I realized in many cases, people who are "available" are "available" for a reason! Perhaps, there is a reason nobody else is going to them for advice.

Sorry for the long story to make my point, but I thought this would also be a good time to inject some personally defacing humor on the scene. By the way, that patio was my last home improvement project!

I hope the next time a situation arises where you're not completely sure you've come up with the best solution, you will seek out the right person, show maturity, set aside your pride, and ask them for help.

*Is there a decision you're currently struggling with that you need to apply this recommendation to?*

## Personal Application

*I Believe I'm always just one bad decision away from doing irreversible damage to myself and potentially others.*

That's a sobering thought. You're probably thinking, *so you are telling me I can make a series of great decisions in my life, and things can be going great, but it only takes one bad decision to wipe my slate clean and I have to start all over?* That is exactly what I'm telling you.

I don't know about you, but the time I start worrying about ole Jack is when things are going really well. Life is good, and I'm enjoying every bit of it. You might as well put a target on my back because that's when I'm most vulnerable to doing something stupid.

It's been said that some people can think they are bulletproof. In other words, things are going so well, nothing can change their momentum and trajectory. They're bulletproof.

- My high school recruit Bill probably thought that at some time in his life.
- Michael Jackson probably did.
- Bill Cosby might have had those thoughts.

- Tiger Woods probably felt that way.
- Richard Nixon could have thought that as well.

None of those people ever in their wildest dreams thought that their life would take the turn it did. I hope you'll keep these names and others that come to mind when you start on your roll. Don't bring out the eraser and wipe your board clean!

I want to close this section on *decisions* or more appropriately *decision-making*, with an idea for you to think about. Decision-making comes down to asking yourself the right questions. If you take the time to think through the right set of questions, it significantly enhances the probability of making a sound decision. Let me make this clear, there is no magic pill that will guarantee you'll always make good decisions. However, there are some steps that will certainly aid in the process, and it is a process.

So the key to good decision-making is the type of questions one considers in analyzing his or her situation. Unfortunately, many times a person tries to think of appropriate questions to ask in working through a decision, but he or she is trying to do so while under the gun to make the decision. That is not the best scenario to do so since in those cases, the person may experience feelings of being rushed. The decision is already upon them, and they are thinking "action" not "process."

Here's what I decided to do, and I hope you'll give it your consideration as well. Before facing any decision, sit down and begin compiling a list of questions that would be somewhat generic in that they could apply in multiple types of situations. Think of any question that comes to mind and just keep a list. After you've compiled your list, you might want to review it and see if you have any questions that are basically asking the same type of question. If so, just remove those from the list.

Once you've purged your list, keep it in a paper file somewhere or on your computer, and when you're faced with your next decision, pull it out and start going through it. If a question doesn't relate to your current situation, skip it and move to the next one. The key is really giving quality time to writing down as many questions as you can that you think could come into play when making a decision. The key is to prepare your list *before* you need it, not *when* you need it.

At the back of your book, you'll see the list I use. For now, I'll give you a few examples to let you see what I'm talking about.

- What are the facts? Do I have enough facts to make this decision? Where can I go to get more information?
- Who might be affected by this decision and how?
- Are there any statements on my *I Believe* list that relates to this decision?

I want to close this section on *decisions* with a few final thoughts.

Sometimes the right or best answer is ambiguous. It's not clear. It just doesn't jump out at you. In fact, that's the case in many decision-making situations. The reason I share that is there is a temptation you need to be on the lookout for. There is the temptation when in doubt to choose to do nothing and not make the decision.

Sometimes putting off a decision is the correct thing to do if it's based on right thinking. But when it's based on the fact that the person won't explore potential options, becomes impatient or fearful, and won't seek the opinions of others, then it's the wrong response. When it comes to decisions, nobody is going to get them all right. This is just not going to happen regardless of how smart or educated you are. But if you will follow the ideas I've shared in this section, you'll definitely improve your results and start making better decisions.

I hope this helps you get the feel of how this process works.

*Now you have some homework to do. Before looking at my list in the back of the book, start working on creating your own list of questions. After you have your list, then go look at mine and add any that you want to put on your list.*

# Personal Application

---

# Takeaways on Decisions

# CHAPTER 4

# Relationships

Treasure your relationships, not your possessions.
—Anthony J D'Angelo

*I Believe in being a good friend and being there when needed—it's a privilege and a responsibility.*

One of my concerns today is with so much interaction via social media and video games, people really don't spend quality time together. You cannot develop really good friends without personal interaction. Likes, selfies, Snapchat, etc., can keep people in touch but in a very superficial way. Friends are developed over time through experiences and personal experiences.

I've been fortunate to have a lot of really good friends. Playing sports obviously helped develop some of these relationships. When you are on an athletic team, you really get a great opportunity to get to know people. You see how they treat others. You see their character. You get a chance to see how genuine they really are.

Being active in church also creates a great opportunity to really get to know someone. You know you have several things in common already through your faith. In addition, being active in your neighborhood or community provides opportunities to get to know people beyond just the superficial, *"How are you today?"* type of relationship.

I feel you truly understand the role of a friend when you move from considering having friends to be a privilege to understanding that friendships come with responsibility. It's easy to be on the receiving end of a friendship, but what about the giving end?

For example, I have a group of college and high school teammates who get together on a regularly scheduled basis. We make it a priority. We do so for the stories and memories and to keep up with what's going on in one another's lives, but we also are there at the hospital when one of them or a family member is having surgery. Because we spend time together on a frequent basis, we also know when one member of the group is "off." They might not seem right. They are saying everything is cool, but their body language says otherwise. That's when our responsibility as a friend needs to kick in. Respectfully, we try to explore a little deeper in order to see what might be going on that is bothering them. Sometimes it calls for a more direct approach and we confront them with our concern.

The tough part of being a friend is when you have to confront one of your friends about something because they need it. They don't want to hear it and may even appear to resent your actions. Down deep, either then or later, they will realize your actions are based on your desire to do what is best for them.

I'm reminded here of the quote by Arnold Glasow, that says, "A true friend never gets in your way unless you happen to be going down."

*When was the last time you sat down and made a list of your true friends? If that's a struggle for you, ask yourself:*

- *What role have I played to develop relationships?*
- *What have I done to do my part in creating relationships?*

*If you have what you consider is a good list, ask yourself, "Do you consider those relationships a privilege and a responsibility?" If not, get to work. It will be time well spent.*

# Personal Application

---

*I Believe in telling people I love them.*

Many people in previous generations were not brought up telling one another they loved them. They felt like their actions should represent that love. In reality, demonstrating your love *is* more important than just telling someone you love them.

My parents were from the generation that showed their love, but you didn't ever hear those magical words come out of their mouths. They would put it in writing, but it wouldn't come out verbally. I was blessed with amazing parents and siblings, and my parents provided my siblings and me with a wonderful heritage. We'll talk later about how important it is to pass on a good name to your children.

I think because my parents' generation was not as comfortable expressing their love verbally, my siblings and I have made up for it with our families and our sibling relationships. We have been blessed as a family, and I think our children and grandchildren have seen each of us express our love not only to them but also to each other on a regular basis. They hear it in our words and see it in our actions.

Family love is one kind of love. What about expressing love to your friends? This next section is primarily focused on the guys reading this book. Men seem to be more hesitant in telling a guy friend that they love them. I was for a long time until one of my teammate friends set me straight.

Smylie Gebhart was two years behind me at Georgia Tech. He was a 6'1" and 195-pound defensive end who earned All-American honors. Smylie and I were not best friends by any means at Tech, other than the bond we had through the football team. Unfortunately, Smylie had a chronic neck problem that he had to deal with all during his playing days. He wore a protective neck brace to give added support the entire time he was playing football.

Several years after he finished playing, Smylie's neck began to cause more discomfort and his doctor recommended having neck surgery. This was back in 1980 and neck surgery, although always dangerous, was not as routine as it is now because of the medical enhancements in that area. Smylie, however, elected to hold off on the surgery. One evening when he was meeting a group of buddies to go to one of their friend's bachelor party, one of the guys was playing around with him, put his arm around him and gave him a big hug. When he did, Smylie's disk ruptured and his spinal cord was severed.

Smylie spent the majority of the next seven years in and out of the hospital as a permanent quadriplegic. Once he was stabilized and able to be at home the majority of the time, a group of his teammates and I started gathering in Atlanta and driving over to Meridian, Mississippi to spend a long weekend with Smylie. The goal was to spend time with Smylie and try to cheer him up. As it turned out, we were the ones that were being motivated and uplifted. Smylie had a way of doing that to people. These trips continued for twenty years until Smylie passed away as a result of a battle with cancer. You talk about a person getting the short end of a stick.

You're probably now thinking, *"Jack, I appreciate you sharing the story about Smylie, and he certainly was a special guy, but what does this have to do with telling someone you love them?"* Glad you asked.

Here's why I shared the story. Smylie would always tell us he loved us when we would leave or speak with him on the phone. I can't speak for the other guys, but I always felt uncomfortable when Smylie would tell me he loved me. I'd always look around to see if anyone heard what he said, hoping they didn't. One day on a phone conversation, Smylie came right out and asked me if it bothered me when he told me he loved me. I wasn't sure how to respond and stumbled around a little with some nonanswer, and he then hit me with the truth serum.

He said, "Jack, do you think I love you?"

I said, "I know you do Smylie."

He then asked me, "Do you love me?"

I said, "You know I do."

He said, "Then I'm going to give you some helpful advice. Get over it!"

I'll never forget the day I got the call that Smylie had passed away or the day I went to Meridian for his funeral. His brother came up to me and said Smylie wanted me to deliver the eulogy. I said, "I'm honored, but please don't ask me to do that. I just don't think I can make it through it." His brother reminded me that Smylie wanted me to do it, and that settled it. I closed my message at the funeral with, "Smylie, I love you."

Don't wait to have to go through a traumatic experience like I did to learn this valuable lesson.

*Who do you need to let know that you love them?*

## Personal Application

*I Believe in telling people I believe in them.*

You might say, Didn't we just cover this above? Yes, there are some similarities, but this is a different type of statement. You can certainly tell people you love that you believe in them. That's almost understood, or at least I hope it is. What I'm referring to in this statement is being sensitive to those people that you interact with and get to know who need encouragement. Sometimes they might need that positive push or need their internal doubt removed.

I get the privilege of working with young people each year in my IDEALS Leadership School. These are high school student athletes, male and female, who are selected by their school and nominated to attend our eight-week program. They are student athletes who have already shown leadership potential, not only with their teams, but also in their respective schools.

Without exception, every year it's very obvious there are a few of these student athletes, not many, who still lack some self-confidence. You wouldn't think that would be the case, because of the fact that their schools selected them to attend because of their leadership potential, but it is. It could be they're struggling with confidence in their athletic ability, their leadership skills or responsibilities, academics, or just in their inter-personal relationships. One of the most rewarding aspects of working with these young people is identifying those that need a reminder that someone believes in them.

*You have people in your life right now who need that same type of encouragement. It could be people you interact with on a regular basis. It could be a family member, teammate, coworker, friend, or neighbor. Put your radar up. Start looking for the signs and then get to work changing their lives for the better.*

*Who comes to mind first?*

# Personal Application

*I Believe I need to spend more time investing in others. Life is all about relationships.*

I hope you already know and agree with this statement. If so, you skip the rest of this narrative. However, before you skip to the next statement on my list, ask yourself, "Are my actions and priorities aligning with my confirmation that I agree with this statement?" If not, you might want to join the others and walk through this topic with us.

I heard a story about a man named Charles Plumb. He was a fighter pilot during the Vietnam War. He was shot down and spent six months in a Vietnamese prison camp. I can't even begin to imagine what that experience might have been like. Once he returned home, he began sharing his stories in talks and lectures around the country, focusing on what he learned through that experience.

He tells the story of sitting in a restaurant with his wife one day when a man approached him and said, "You're Plumb. You flew jet fighters in Vietnam. You were shot down."

Plumb asked, "How in the world did you know that?"

The man replied, "I packed your parachute."

Plumb gasped in surprise and gratitude. Then the man pumped his fist and said, "I guess it worked!"

Plumb responded, "It sure did. If your chute hadn't worked, I wouldn't be here today."

Plumb wondered if he had ever seen that man before and had no idea how he had impacted his life.

You see, when we spend time investing in the lives of others, we are "packing their parachute." Think about the people who invested in you and what that meant to you over your life. Think about all the ways they invested in you.

How do we invest in people?

- Give of our time
- Show an interest in what they are doing
- Encourage them when they seem stuck or discouraged
- Be there when they need someone to talk to
- Listen more than you talk when you're with them
- Be there when they think they don't need someone to talk to, but they do
- Share your experiences

A friend of mine, John Vaughn, wrote a book called *The Accountability Changes Everything Journal*. It's a journal that each day asks you to answer one question. I'm not a person who keeps a journal; however, I wish I did because I see the benefit in doing so, but up until now, that just hasn't been a priority for me. That being said, I knew I could make the time to answer one question each morning. Boy, what a great resource that journal has been for me. I highly recommend it to you.

One day, one of the questions really stunned me. The question was a simple one. "Who do you need to spend more time with?" Immediately, two people jumped out. I mean it happened in a nanosecond.

My thoughts were, *If these people came to mind so quickly, why haven't I been spending more time with them?* I didn't have an answer, but I did have a response. My response was to immediately pick up the phone and reach out to them and set up a time to get together.

I am glad to report that those two individuals are now seeing a lot more of me whether they like it or not.

The first thing to do is to understand the value of investing in others. Second, be on the lookout for those who need a "deposit of your time and interest." Third, don't worry about what to do next. You'll know what to do.

*Who are some people who invested in you and really made a positive impact on your life? Have you told them how much their investment has meant to you?*

*Who do you need to spend more time with?*

## Personal Application

---

*I Believe in forgiveness—for me, by me of others, and forgiving myself.*

Forgiveness. *Whew!* That's not a word we spend a lot of time talking about, is it? Why not? Because it takes a lot of work, and it often seems unfair to let that person off the hook that hurt you or treated you wrong.

If you look closely at that statement, I refer to three types of forgiveness. The first one says forgiveness for me. That makes the assumption that I need forgiving for something I did or something maybe I should have done and didn't do. News flash! This not only applies to me, but it could also apply to you.

There's only been one person who walked this earth that didn't need forgiving, and I'll let you in on a secret—it's not you or me. In fact, the first part of this *I Believe* statement relates to that person and His relationship with me. I believe I have been forgiven of my sins because Christ died on a cross for them. He bore the penalty of my sins so I wouldn't have to. I start with that forgiveness first instead of the other two because it is the *most* important one in my life.

The first part of the *I Believe* statement also applies to others forgiving me when I have done something inappropriate and have hurt them. If I took the time to make a list of things I *know* I did that needed forgiveness, this book would have to be reclassified as a novel.

The second part of the statement relates to me forgiving others who have done something to hurt me in some way. If you live a life of any length, you are unfortunately going to have people do regretful things to you, and you are going to have people in your life that make bad choices that can negatively impact others, and one of those others may be you. It's going to happen. Sometimes these actions are designed to hurt. Other times, people do things and really don't mean to hurt others, but ultimately do. The thought process or intent is irrelevant. I need to forgive these people just like Christ forgave me.

I think the final component to this *I Believe* statement is the hardest. I know Christ has forgiven me, and I'm trying my best to forgive others who have, in my opinion, hurt me. The problem I have is being willing to forgive myself for some of the stupid, terrible things I've done that not only negatively impacted my life but also the lives of others—the lives of people I care about and love. It's that novel I mentioned above.

I don't think I am alone with this problem. I think most people keep harboring that anxiety, frustration, and regret associated with things they have done, and frequently ask themselves, "What was I thinking? How could I have done that?"

It's a heavy anchor to carry around for the rest of your life. I'm going to share a personal story that relates to this area a little later on when I talk about learning from the past but not dwelling there.

Let's wrap this up by asking these questions: *Who do you need to forgive that you just haven't been able to bring yourself to do so? What are some things you have done in your life that you keep beating yourself up about and need to forgive yourself and move on?*

*Finally and most importantly, have you asked Christ to forgive you of your sins?*

## Personal Application

---

*I Believe I need to overlook the small stuff in relationships.*

Let me quickly clarify what I'm not referring to in this statement. I'm not talking about ignoring the little things that are important in relationships—those things that people appreciate you doing for them that they didn't ask you to do, the things that aren't major but are still appreciated. I'm not talking about those actions.

What I am talking about are those "little things" people do that might irritate you but are not really that important in the grand scheme of life.

I'll share a simple example. My wife has long hair. I have hair that has a very wide part in the middle or, more simply stated, bald. Hair is both important to me from a vanity standpoint and an irritant when left around in sinks and counters or on food. Let's eliminate the reference to food because that truly is disgusting! My wife has a tendency to blow dry her hair on my side of the bathroom vanity because the light is better. When she does, there is always what I refer to as "escaped prisoners" who are trying to make a run for it. In other words, hairs that fall around the sink.

When I go to brush my teeth, the first things I see are these "runaways." It drives me crazy because I don't like to see hairs anywhere but on someone's head, preferably mine. For a long time, each day I'd ask my wife if she would clean up behind herself and get the hairs out of the sink and off the counter. It became a daily ritual and quite frankly, not the best way to start either of our days.

Finally, I realized how silly this was. Yes, the hairs irritated me, and I had a right to mention it to my wife, but was this something so monumental that it was worth starting both of our days on a negative note? My other option was to not say a word and simply clean up the hairs before I did whatever I was going to do in my area of the vanity. As you might expect, the latter option has become a much better choice for both of us. Just so you don't think your author is some type of martyr, I will have you know that my wife has chosen to do the same thing with some of the things I do to irritate her but are not "marriage threatening."

That is a simple example of what I'm referring to. In every relationship, there are major things that come up, and there are minor things. Make life better for all. Choose your battles, let the minor stuff slide, and stay focused on the major things.

*Here's your challenge for this statement: What are some things that people may do or a specific person may do that have been bugging you? Are these things you really need to just overlook and not make such a big issue, and move on?*

# Personal Application

*I Believe in treating people with dignity and respect, and not being judgmental.*

This statement is a mixed bag for me. This statement usually has one of those asterisks by it that indicates I need to focus more on aligning my actions with my statement. On the other hand, there is something I do related to this statement that I feel really good about. Let me explain.

One of my faults that I'm trying to get better at is judging others. I have a bad habit of quickly judging someone by the way they look, what they wear, or how they might conduct themselves. Now I don't even know anything about this person, but I've already "studied" their life and decided they are such and such.

Let me give you an example. You will find out, if you haven't already, I'm a very transparent person. I feel we grow as a country when each person is honest about our biases. We can't work toward appropriate solutions without first admitting the problem and the role each of us plays in either the creation or perpetuation of a problem. I hope the example I share doesn't offend those who might fit the example I'm going to use. Please make sure you read this section all the way through before forming your thoughts on what I believe. I'm just being honest and sharing, as I like to say, "An opinion of one," and how I feel about it. Now that I have acknowledged my disclaimer, that which I am well aware will not hold up in court, let me share my example.

My wife and I are walking down the street, and we see someone on the sidewalk or street asking for money, and my judgmental radar kicks in. It's irrelevant to me what race or nationality this person is. That is not a contributing factor to my reaction. I've already come to the conclusion that they are worthless, don't want to work, a taker, never will amount to anything, and are going to use the money for alcohol. My thoughts escalate if they are wearing their pants around their thighs and have tats all over their body. I think I've covered everything in my quiver of judgmental thoughts. I will immediately try to maneuver to the other side of the street to avoid the confrontation for fear I might say something I'll regret later.

My wife, on the other hand, has just the opposite reaction to that type of situation. She will go out of her way and drag me along with her to give that person some money. When I say give that person some money, I'm not talking about a dollar. Oh no, she doesn't want us to short-change this person. She'll pull out a five or larger and give it to them. That woman has cost me a lot of money, but she is *right*, and I am *wrong* in how I handle that situation.

Before we leave this example, I also want to share something else I've learned. Through my wife's influence and actions, I've also been surprised by how many times my "analysis" of that person proved me wrong. Because of this, I'm happy to say, I'm doing much better in this area.

Now before you throw me under the bus or toss this book aside in disgust at how I handle that type of situation, let me share the other aspect of this statement that I handle much better.

I really have a passion for going up to people who are doing jobs that many people would prefer not to do or maybe stronger, wouldn't do, but are important and need to be done. One that comes to mind immediately is those special people who serve in the role of custodians in schools, businesses, or other types of buildings. Many of their daily tasks are not something I'd like to wake up and go to work to do. I clean the bathrooms in my house, but I wouldn't want to do so in a public place as they are required to do.

I try to make it a point when I see someone doing a task like that to go up to them and ask if they realize how important what they are doing is and tell them I appreciate what they do. I am sincere with both parts of my comment.

Let me give you a good example, and my wife is in this one as well.

Being a former athlete and becoming more former every day, I still try to work out at least five days a week, sometimes six. I've been doing that for a long time. My wife—yes, that benevolent woman who helps those in need—abhors working out.

I had just changed gyms, and the first day I went in, I saw a woman cleaning the workout area. I immediately went up to her, introduced myself, and asked her if she knew how important the work she was doing was. She really didn't respond, just nodded. She was Hispanic and struggled with her English. I followed that by asking what her name was and told her I appreciated the work she does, and she was doing a great job. Her name was Alba.

I came home that day and told my wife about Alba. Well, a lightning bolt came down from the sky that day, and my wife decided she wanted to join that gym and start working out.

Let me stop here and share some pertinent history on this subject. I already mentioned she does not like to work out, but she has attempted it at several gyms. Usually, those gyms require a one to two-year membership fee. Unfortunately, she rarely goes more than four to five times, then stops. Did I mention that my wife has cost me a lot of money?

After interrogating her about whether or not she really wanted to do this again, join a gym that is, she said she did. On the first day we went together, I introduced her to Alba, and they talked briefly. On the second trip that we went together, which also would go down as her last day (see previous paragraph), I mentioned I didn't see Alba. My wife said she was working in the ladies' restroom. She then said Alba told her something that really floored me. Alba told her that she had been working at the gym for about six months, and I was the only gym member that even spoke to her, much less thanked her for the work she did to keep our gym a clean and healthy place to work out.

That really got to me. It's tragic, but it happens all the time. So often, we walk by people like Alba, ignore them, and don't take the time to let them know we appreciate what they do. When you do take the time to do so, watch their face brighten when you share those words. The Albas of the world are all around us. They are not just custodians. They are anyone doing a job that you wouldn't want to do but is necessary and one you appreciate them doing.

*Start keeping your eyes open for the opportunity to let someone know you appreciate what they do and watch how those simple words impact their day. The "Albas" are waiting for you and need you. Who comes to mind?*

## Personal Application

# Takeaways on Relationships

# CHAPTER 5

# Character

When wealth is lost, nothing is lost; when health is lost,
something is lost; when character is lost, all is lost!

—Anonymous

*I Believe in establishing a good name and preserving it through my actions.*

One of the most important things a person can do during their life is to establish a good name and pass that name down to their children. Some of us have been very fortunate, in that we inherited a great name. Others, however, are having to overcome the mistakes of previous generations and must start to work through that and create a positive name to pass on to their children.

There is a lot of talk today about "brands." Companies have brands. Brands are designed to help people have the thought, perception, or image that the company wants you to have about their company, product, or service. Companies spend millions of dollars to try to influence your perception of a particular image so that your perception of the company meets the brand image they desire. For instance, just think about how much companies pay for a thirty-second ad during the Super Bowl.

People have brands too. A person's brand is what people think of when they see that person or hear the person's name. It's that simple. You and I right now have a brand based on that definition. It may be good or bad based on many factors we control.

Let's look for a minute at things we do every day that can either develop or destroy our brand. Things like:

- The decisions we make
- How we treat people
- What we say or what we don't say
- Who we spend time with
- How we handle success
- How we handle adversity
- The language we use
- How we spend our time
- How we spend our money
- What we watch or don't watch on TV, movies, Internet, etc.
- How we define what success looks like in our life
- Our actions aligning with what we say is important

*Everything on that list you can control. So if you are going to establish a good name, what do you need to start doing, stop doing, or continue doing to be able to do so?*

## Personal Application

---

*I believe in being a positive role model.*

Just like having a brand, each one of us is a role model for someone. We normally associate the term role model as being a positive term. But that is only the goal. A lot has to happen for that to occur. A lot of the things we mentioned above about establishing a great name apply to this statement. By definition, a role model is someone others can look up to. They want to be like them. This can mean different things to different people, depending on who the role model is and who the person is that wants to be like them.

In our country, many of the role models of our youth have changed over the years. A generation or so ago, role models were parents, ministers, business leaders, politicians, etc. Today, most of the young people want to emulate are celebrities—professional athletes, musicians, movie stars, etc. Why do you think so many companies seek these people to be spokespersons for their products? Think about how much Nike gear Michael Jordan sold for that company. If you pay attention to what young people are wearing, you will often notice that their clothes, shoes, and accessories are directly influenced by these public figures.

I wonder how much time parents today actually think about how their actions are influencing their children. With all the pressure on parents today because of careers, hobbies, and commitments, less and less time is being focused on the part they play as positive role models for their children. When you think about the number of single-parent households out there and the added responsibilities that role entails, this just complicates the task.

Every single one of us has a sphere of influence—both direct and indirect—who are influenced by our actions. Some people in our sphere are extremely obvious, and at other times, they are not. The example I gave of celebrities is an example of people being in their indirect sphere of influence. These personalities don't interface or interact with these young people personally, but their actions, behavior, and lifestyles are indirectly influencing them.

Not only does each of us have our sphere of influence we impact, but we are also in other people's spheres of influence. Those people can also influence us, either directly or indirectly. Role models are not just parents; they are teachers, business leaders, friends, neighbors, coaches, public safety representatives, etc. There is not a position or role today in which a person cannot serve as a positive role model for others. Let me emphasize, we need role models for adults just as we do for young people.

- A husband and wife who set a great example of what a marriage should look like
- A father or mother who set an example for other mothers and fathers of how positive parenting works
- A businessperson who demonstrates in their business dealings how an ethical person in business thinks and acts
- A brother or sister who demonstrates how to be a good sibling

There is one other key point for our younger readers. Don't think for a minute that as a young person, you can't be a positive role model for adults. I know of numerous situations where children have been truly positive role models in the lives of their parents. In addition, teachers will tell you that they've had students impact their lives very positively in ways that the students could never imagine.

The examples are endless.

*The question is, Who is in your sphere of influence and what type of influence are you making in their lives? Start your list.*

## Personal Application

---

*I Believe in being aware of the habits in my life—both positive and negative.*

News flash. People are creatures of habit. We all have our habits and routines. Some are good habits, and some are not. Some people try to fool themselves into thinking otherwise but those who know them can quickly dispel that unfounded thought.

Personally, I have some habits I'd like to change. My wife would tell you quickly that I need to take smaller bites of food when I eat. Maybe that is just bad etiquette. Regardless, I do it habitually.

One habit I have is I eat the same thing for breakfast 99 percent of the time: a mixture of Cheerios and Wheat Chex. Don't ask me how I got started on that combo. The breakfast includes bananas on the cereal, watermelon, in season or not, and a toasted English muffin. I down that wonderful meal with a bottle of water. Each and every day, that is the breakfast of champions in the Williams's household.

Let's get serious for a minute, though, regarding habits. Habits are just like the compound effect of interest on money. When I share this topic of habits in a live seminar, I get two people to volunteer for a quick exercise.

I give one of them a choice to take either $5 million now or a penny a day that doubles every day for thirty days. It's interesting the logic they use in making the first choice.

Then we start the comparison over time. As you can imagine, the person that has the $5 million is feeling pretty good as we do a comparison in ten-day intervals and reach the twenty-day mark. But at day 30, the penny a day choice passes the $5 million mark, and then remember it doubles one more day. Consequently, that choice results in approximately $10 million in thirty-one days.

The point I like to make is this is the same thing that can happen with habits. Habits can compound over time.

Assume you have a bad habit and you know it's bad, but you just haven't chosen to stop it. Your logic is you know it's bad, but it really hasn't hurt you yet, so you continue to do it. Then over time, just like the compound interest example, that habit's impact continues to increase and significantly affects you in a negative way.

You're thinking, gosh, I did not see that coming. Well, you should have. You knew what you were doing was wrong. Over time, what didn't seem to be a big thing became a BIG thing. Did you think you weren't going to have to pay a price at some point?

A similar problem can occur when you have a good habit. Let's say you have a good habit that you know is a positive one, and you want to keep doing it. Unfortunately, maybe it's one that takes a while for you to fully reap the benefit of your actions. Again, it's like the compound effect of interest. The real "payday" takes a while to develop. Sometimes people get discouraged and think that this good habit was going to really pay dividends, and yet they haven't seen any significant benefit, so they stop whatever it was they were doing. Unfortunately, many times, they stop that habit right before the compound effect (positive benefit) was going to kick in.

*The question I want you to think about is, What bad habit do you need to stop doing before it negatively affects you? What is a good habit you're doing right now that you know is the right thing to do but hasn't quite gotten to the point of really benefitting you yet?*

## Personal Application

*I Believe in personal accountability.*

I am going to share again what I like to say is "an opinion of one" with you. I think one of the single biggest differences in our country over the last seventy years (basically a generation) has been the decline of personal accountability.

Our country was built by previous generations who took personal responsibility and accountability seriously. They took pride in their work and thought through their decisions because they knew their name was going to be associated with it. They owned their actions.

Today, we don't see that type of mentality or mindset or at least not as much as we did in the past. Anytime something goes wrong, people are looking to lay blame on someone, and that someone is never themselves.

We see over and over a person or organization that makes a mistake, and instead of accepting responsibility for that mistake, they chooses to try to cover it up. Usually, the cover-up gets them in deeper trouble than the original mistake. When is the last time you heard somebody say, *"I messed up. My fault. My bad,"* then correct it and move on? The silence is killing me. We have to get back to stepping up and taking responsibility for our actions and get out of the excuse and blame game.

*What area of your life do you need to step up and start being more accountable and accepting responsibility?*

## Personal Application

---

*I Believe in doing what I say I'm going to do or what I know I should do.*

I could have easily thrown this statement in the accountability bucket and covered it there, but I think this one needs special attention. At least it does for me.

Unfortunately, today people stand out or positively differentiate themselves simply by doing what they say they are going to do. That is tragic, but it's so much the exception today rather than the norm. When I was leading people in business, this was one of the first traits I looked for in the people that worked with me and for me. I wanted to know who I could depend on.

The statement on my original *I Believe* list stopped at "I Believe in doing what I say I'm going to do." I added the second point "or what I know I should do" several years later. I can honestly say there have been many weeks after I added that last part of the statement that I wished I hadn't done so. In fact, of all the items on my list, this one raises its ugly head more often than the others.

Here's what I'm talking about. I'm pretty good about doing what I say I'm going to do. However, there are times when I said I would attend some event or do something, and when the time came around to actually do it, other things began to complicate the issue. Perhaps my day got changed, for it might have been an evening event, and I was exhausted at the end of the day and didn't want to do another thing.

Have you ever experienced that? Many times, it really isn't something significant. Maybe I said I would be there to support a friend, and there are going to be a lot of people at that event, and maybe they won't even notice if I'm not there. This single statement has dragged my rear to more events, meetings, and activities than I would like to admit.

The second part of the *I Believe* statement has also placed a guilt trip on me on numerous occasions. For instance, there is something I didn't commit to and maybe wasn't even asked to get involved, but I knew I should have. Again, my schedule was tight or as I said earlier, I was tired. However, down deep, I knew the right thing to do was to go or be there. As much as I've muttered an unflattering word under my breath and sometimes audibly, as I'm walking out the door when I didn't want to, I'm grateful this statement is on my list. It has made me a better person by being there.

I remember having breakfast with Homer Rice, the legendary football coach and college Athletic Director. His wife had been in a nursing home for some time, and recently her health had declined to the point that she didn't even recognize him or know he was there. He had a daily routine that he would go and sit with his wife from 9:00 a.m. to 2:00 p.m. each day. I may have the hours off a little, but he went daily and not just for an hour.

He shared at breakfast that a friend had asked him, "Why does he still go when she doesn't even know who you are anymore?" His response was typical Homer Rice, which has made him the man he is. Homer said, "She may not know who I am, but I know who she is."

*How are you doing in this category? Do you need to have this type of statement on your list to remind you of what is really important?*

## Personal Application

---

*I Believe in patience, persistence, and perseverance.*

Today, everybody wants things now—fast food, Internet speed, promotions, money, etc. We are constantly being told we deserve all of this. The fact is we don't. We don't "deserve" anything. We have been conditioned to expect these things, but that doesn't necessarily mean we deserve them. It has been said patience is a virtue. Today it really is. To get anything worthwhile takes patience, persistence, and perseverance. Anything of value doesn't come quickly or easily or without effort, setbacks, and sacrifice.

Let me share a personal story to demonstrate this. After I left the coaching profession, I went to work for a paper company. I was in training to go into sales when I began to be recruited by a major life insurance company. After several months of discussions, I decided to make the change and get into the world of insurance. You want to talk about a "friend killer." Let people know you're going into the life insurance business. But honestly, it's a much-needed product, and we all should take that responsibility seriously. That said, it was a really tough road trying to get started. I worked with a great trainer and had a great company to work for, but I can't begin to tell you how many hang-ups and "not interested" comments I received.

They teach you when you're just starting out to write down everybody you know and start with them. I did what they told me to do. I found it interesting how many fewer Christmas cards I received after I got into the insurance business!

Well, I had a former teammate at Georgia Tech whose father and another man had started a uniform rental business. The father had bought out his partner, and now he and his two sons owned the business. The company rented eleven sets of work uniforms to its customers' employees. Each week, they would deliver five sets of clean clothes, pick up five dirty sets, and the employees would wear what they called the "eleventh change." Little did I know that five years later, I would start a fourteen-year career in the uniform rental industry.

I approached my former teammate about their company's insurance needs. He was a year younger than I was and especially bright. We were not real close friends in college but were still teammates. Ironically, I was his host when we were recruiting him. That's a story that, for all parties involved, needs to remain untold.

So we have all heard the statement, "I'd rather be lucky than good." Well, I was about to find out exactly what that meant. When I called on him and finally was able to get in front of him, he realized that he, his brother, and dad all needed life insurance coverage related to the business and their estates. I tried to remain calm and acted as if this was an everyday experience for me. By that I mean, someone realizing they actually needed insurance!

As we began to talk about what the need was and how much insurance would be required to cover the need, I began to get a little lightheaded. We agreed that each one of them needed $1 million of coverage! Little did I know that this was going to be the easy part.

I had countless meetings with my former teammate, the older son. He agreed there was a need, and we actually got all three members of the family to complete the application and get the required physicals. That's a pretty strong sign the deal is going to go through. Unfortunately, both the father and the oldest son, my contact, hated to put anything in writing. I was pleasantly surprised when they finally completed and signed the life insurance application.

The father and my former teammate were historically slow decision-makers. In the life insurance business, the deal is not finalized until the client makes a payment for at least the first month's premium for the coverage. This is where I experienced their propensity to go slow in pulling the trigger on the deal. I focused all of my efforts on my former teammate to get his dad on board with the expectation the younger brother was going to follow the lead of his dad and older brother.

I would make an appointment to meet with my teammate and have to wait for up to three hours sometimes to see him. He was in the building but was apparently preoccupied with other things and used that as a way to avoid finalizing the policies. Other times, he would cancel at the last minute. It was *really* frustrating.

This behavior continued for several months. I kidded with the receptionist of his company who had seen me numerous times sitting in their waiting area, that I had qualified for their pension plan based on my time of "service" to the company—waiting time.

I decided to get creative. My teammate didn't live too far from me and I knew he was going out of town. I came up with the idea to create some messaging on three poster boards. I was going to drive up to his house and nail them on his big front porch. I thought he might get a kick out of my creativity and effort, and maybe that would finally move the needle.

The night I decided to do it turned out to be a night that I was in serious danger and didn't even know it. I thought his wife was out of town as well, and no one was home. They lived back in some woods in a very secluded area. Later, my teammate told me the night I went up there and nailed the posters to the porch, his wife was home and had me in her sights with her shotgun the whole time!

Nevertheless, my creativity with the poster board and placing my life in danger did not change the decision-making process to finalize the $3 million life insurance deal. Because of this last setback, I was seriously wondering whether this deal was going to happen. My boss back at the insurance company kept pushing me to close the deal, which added to the frustration. I was doing everything I was trained to do, and a few things that weren't in the training manual.

Finally, I had a do or die idea. I felt there was a high probability the deal wasn't going to happen, so I got bolder with my next move. I decided to send him a letter that started Dear (Teammate's name) and then I left the body of the letter blank leaving enough room for potentially three to four short paragraphs. I then closed the letter, sincerely Jack Williams. Below my signature at the bottom of the page, I wrote in ink, "Thought I'd summarize the progress we've made over the last three months!"

The day he received the letter, I got a call. He was laughing saying, "I got him on that one." A week later, I closed the deal on a $3 million life insurance sale.

Post note to that story—I got so much attention as a rookie salesman closing that size of sale that I decided I wanted to specialize in "big" sales. I simply didn't take into consideration that I had a strong relationship with the prospect, that there was a real need, and maybe the most important fact, I got really lucky.

In my quest to specialize in "big" sales, I nearly went broke and ironically ended up going to work for the client that bought the $3 million policy. How about that for a Paul Harvey, "rest of the story."

It's going to take strong patience, persistence, and perseverance if you're going to accomplish worthwhile things in your life. However, if you can ingrain the "Three Ps" in your value system, great days are ahead for you.

*What are some things right now that call for patience, persistence, and perseverance in your life?*

## Personal Application

---

*I Believe I have the same amount of time as everyone else—10,080 minutes each week. It's my responsibility to plan and prioritize it.*

I've said it, you've said it, we've all said it: "I didn't have enough time."

Let's look for a second at some of the variables or factors that can negatively affect how someone uses their time.

- Procrastination
- Feeling overwhelmed
- Poor organization—no plan
- Laziness
- Not dealing with reality
- Being reactive rather than proactive
- Underestimating how long something will take
- Not being prepared to start
- Interruptions

- Lack of self-discipline
- Social media temptations

How many items on this list can we actually control? I'd say all of them, with maybe the exception being interruptions. There are also ways we can handle interruptions in a professional manner as well, so we can reduce their impact too.

The first thing we all have to understand is that we are not some victim when it comes to managing our time. I actually even hate to use the word managing because that's a word that can intimidate some people. It's just not that hard. It's all about planning and then prioritizing our time.

If you have trouble in this area, just start thinking of classifying all your activities into one of four categories—Must Do, Should Do, Like to Do, and Caution Do.

*Must Do* activities are just what it sounds like. They are things that are not optional. You must do them. Some can be regular activities such as work, school, or sleep, and others can be things that come up that must have your attention.

*Should Do* are things that you should do, but you don't have to do right now. They are not pressing. Working on a project ahead of the due date. Studying for a test prior to the night before. Exercising. Spending time with family.

*Like to Do* are things you like to do, but you don't have to do. They are not pressing either. These can be fun things in your life like spending time with friends, entertainment, video games, etc.

*Caution Do* are those things that if you spend too much time doing, they negatively affect you. Some of these can be *Like to Do* activities done in excess, such as video games, TV, and social media. Nothing is wrong with doing things you like to do, but they have to be in balance.

All right, now it's time for you to think about the fact that you control almost all the variables that can negatively impact your time. Accept that truth and start planning and prioritizing your time more wisely.

*What are some changes you can start making right now to do a better job planning and prioritizing your time?*

## Personal Application

---

*I Believe in taking care of myself physically, spiritually, and emotionally.*

I already shared I have a tendency to be judgmental. One of the things that upsets me is when people don't take care of themselves physically. There are diseases that can hit anybody at any time; we all know that. I've pledged to do my part not to let a health issue arise that I could have prevented by doing the basic things we can all do to take care of ourselves.

Being a former athlete is one driver of this belief. Self-discipline and dedication, by-products of participating in sports, also play a role in this being a priority in my life. However, you don't have to be a college athlete to take care of yourself physically. It's a mindset.

Using my earlier example on time, I moved taking care of myself physically from the *Should Do* to a *Must Do* category. I make it a priority and build it into my day. You can too, regardless of what type of work you do. There *is* time. There are so many ways you can exercise, and you don't have to have all the latest equipment or go to a gym. That said, making the financial commitment to join a gym is a good step in making this a priority. Just make sure you are going to go if you sign one of those multiyear deals!

It's important to take care of myself spiritually and emotionally as well. Faith is a big part of my life. I stepped away from it during a period of my life, and I made some decisions I truly regret. We'll talk about some of those later in the book.

I have a group of scriptures, probably sixty or so, that I review each week. I have each one on a three-by-five card and break them into five days, Monday through Friday. Each morning, I start the day reading the scriptures assigned for that day. I also have a targeted group of people or things that I pray for designated by day. I've already mentioned earlier that I start each Monday with reading my *I Believe* list then follow that with scriptures and conclude by praying for that day's targeted group.

I also like to conclude my day with a devotional or general scripture reading. My objective is to start and end my day focused on strengthening my faith.

Taking care of myself emotionally is really a by-product of a lot of the other statements on my list. If my actions consistently support my belief statements emotionally, I should be on solid ground. That does not mean I completely avoid having those "days" like everyone else has, where things just seem out of sync. I've just found they are just fewer of those days, and it is easier to bounce back from them when they do occur.

I've shared what I like to do and the type of routine that best works for me. Your routine may be different. The key is to establish a routine that will make these three areas of your life a true priority.

*What are some steps you can begin to take to gain a better balance in these three areas of living a healthy life?*

# Personal Application

---

# Takeaways on Character

# CHAPTER 6

# Communication



> The single biggest problem in communication
> is the illusion that it has taken place.
> —George Bernard Shaw

Mr. Shaw lived around a hundred years ago when he made this statement. You would think over a hundred years we might have improved. Sadly, though, we all know that hasn't happened.

*I Believe in being a good listener—showing respect to the other person talking.*

I mentioned earlier that when I struggle with one of my statements, I put as asterisk by it as a reminder I need to focus on doing better in this area. Well, here is one of those statements. I still struggle with this particularly with a very important person in my life—my wife. Oh, by the way, for those who are married, this is not the person I'd recommend struggling with in this area, but it is in my case.

Ironically when I was leading a major division in a Fortune 500 company, I'd like to think that others would have given me a really high grade in my listening skills. I really do. I made a concerted effort to actually try to understand what they were saying and even more importantly, why they were saying it. Another quick point on listening. Listening to try to get a feel for what someone is not saying is taking listening to the next level. Hope you followed that.

I've found just because a person says something, that doesn't necessarily mean that's what they really mean. Sometimes people feel safer by simply saying what the other person wants to hear. They get in less trouble doing that. That's not a healthy relationship, whether it is work or personal; however, unfortunately, it's certainly not an uncommon practice.

The frustrating part for me is somehow when I come home and walk through the door, my listening skills stay in the car. My wife will be speaking to me about something, and I know she's talking because her lips are moving, but I have no clue what's coming out of her mouth. It's terribly disrespectable to my wife. I know it is, but I still struggle with it.

It might help here to look at the different types of listening a person can choose to use. These are three types of listening. First, there is listening to understand. This is the gold standard for listening. You are giving the other person your full attention and are focusing on making sure you hear everything they say correctly. Unfortunately, this is rarely executed.

The second type of listening is when a person appears to be genuinely listening, but what they are really doing is waiting for the other person to finish so they can share what they want to talk about. Let's refer to this as fake listening.

Finally, the third kind is when a person is listening and hoping the speaker either pauses or takes a breath so they can interrupt and tell them why they disagree with what the other person is saying. I refer to that type of listening as listening to rebut.

Let's put this listening thing in a situation that we can all relate to. We all know when someone is really not paying attention to us when we're speaking to them. It could be their eyes, their body language, or they are trying to multi-task and do other things while they are supposed to be listening. How does that make you feel when someone does that to you? Not very good. I've been on both ends of that equation. I try to use these situations as a motivating factor to improve as a listener.

I want to close on a positive note and not let you think my wife and I are about to go our separate ways. I'm still struggling, but here is what I've started doing to get better. When I find myself not listening while she is speaking, I get up and go right to where she is. I fess up and say, "Honey, I really apologize. I wasn't paying attention." I look her straight in her eyes and ask her if she would please start over because I know what she is saying is important or she wouldn't be sharing it with me. Okay, sometimes I may be stretching the truth a little with that statement. *I listen with my eyes.* When you are standing in front of someone who is speaking to you, it's really hard not to pay attention. The one who is speaking especially appreciates it because you stopped what you were doing, got up, and showed you are sincerely making the effort to do better.

Just in case I get slack in this area with my wife, flowers also help!

*Which of the three types of listeners are you? Who do you need to start standing in front of when they speak and start listening with your eyes?*

## Personal Application

---

*I Believe in understanding the difference in teaching and telling.*

You might be wondering, How did this statement get on this list? I am going to share one last short sports story; I promise this will be the last one and it will be short.

Once again, this story's origin occurred during from my coaching days at Virginia. After we had once again lost the previous day's game, I was reviewing a game film early one Sunday morning. Coaches spend Sundays reviewing game film and grading each player on their performance. Afterward, each coach gets with their respective players and reviews their performances with them. Any coach will tell you, if they are honest, it sure is easier to grade a player's performance after a win than it is a loss. Unfortunately, at Virginia, we didn't get to test that theory very often, and this Sunday was no exception.

I was playing the film backward and forward to be able to accurately assess everything that was happening on each play and how my quarterback was executing. As I was doing so, I noticed on one of the plays I was reviewing that the quarterback had made a mental mistake, which resulted in a bad play. I was in the process of finishing the review of that specific play when the head coach walked in and quickly noticed that same mistake.

He walked up to me and said, "What in the world is he doing?"

Being the sharp coach that I thought I was, I quickly said very confidently, "Coach, I've told him and told him and told him, when the defense does this, you have to do this." The fact was I had done just that.

Our head coach got a little closer to me. The kind of close where you can smell his breath. He then proceeded to say very slowly and carefully to make sure I understood the exact meaning of the "coaching" I was about to receive, "I don't give a flip how many times you told him. It's clearly obvious you didn't teach him!"

He was 100 percent right.

I never forgot that coaching moment because it applies equally in any aspect of our lives, not just coaching football. You see I wrongly made the assumption that repeatedly telling someone something equated to them learning what I wanted them to learn. Sometimes that works with some folks, but it's a weak argument.

I really saw this issue come into play during my time leading people in the business world. Here's what I found out to be the secret in transitioning from telling to teaching. You have to anticipate the questions that are going through people's mind when you are asking them to do something. I believe most people want to follow directions. In other words, you have to consider this. If you were on the other side of the instructions, what questions in your head would you be thinking that needed answering. In studying this situation, I have come up with what I like to call the "five-step communication tree." I use it when I am trying to get someone to do something or buy into what I'm asking him or her to do. Here are the five simple steps.

First, you have to be very specific in telling them what you want them to do. They will not buy into vague ideas or instructions. You have to do your homework to be able to be very specific with what you want them to accomplish. Let me emphasize, very specific.

Second, you have to tell them why this is important. Why is it going to be worth the effort you're asking them to exert?

Third, make sure you are honest and share with them what it's going to take. This is where a lot of people drop the ball. Let's say, what you want them to do is going to take significant effort. The leader gets concerned that if he or she really shares what it's going to take, the group may not buy in and do it. What the leader isn't thinking about is, What if he tells them it's not going to be that hard and they agree to do it and then quickly realize the leader misled them? That leader has lost credibility, not only for that task, but for future ones as well. Be honest in sharing what is going to be required to do the job.

Let me share a side story that exposed me to this problem at an early age. When I was around ten to eleven years old, my dad wanted to have bonding time on some Saturdays. My definition of bonding turned out to be significantly different than my dad's definition. Bonding to him meant working in the yard!

What do you think was my first question when I heard this "exciting" news? You got it. "Dad, how long is this going to take?" Here I was an active young boy who had a full slate of activities planned for the day, and now I've been told part of that day is no longer mine to plan. His standard answer was "only a couple of hours." Well, let me tell you it *never* was a couple of hours. It was usually four to five hours. As these bonding days continued and my dad's habit of miscalculating the time required, it kind of became a joke between the two of us. But when it's not a father-son situation where this occurs, it will never be viewed as funny.

Next, explain to them how this benefits the company, team, project, etc. followed by how it benefits them personally. Human nature always is going to pose the mental question, "How is this going to affect me?" If that's a question the recipient is thinking, then as a leader or teacher, you have to address that upfront, before they bring it up internally.

Remember, you can lose credibility as a leader by not being transparent about the effort that is going to be required. You have the opportunity to gain credibility as a leader by anticipating the questions your people are thinking and covering them in your instructions.

Finally, there are two simple questions you need to ask the person or group you are leading or instructing. Did I miss anything? Are there any questions?

Too often a leader will relay his or her instructions, and actually the message may be pretty clear, but not totally clear. The leader might make the assumption that he or she covered everything, yet those two questions were never asked.

Now to follow this communication tree model, it forces the leader to do their homework. They have to put in the effort on the front-end so they don't have to deal with the corrections and time wasted on the back end by not doing so.

A leader has to be able to clearly handle the first four steps. If a leader cannot clearly state what's needed in those first four steps, then stop the presses. Don't go any further. Their efforts are not going to be successful. The people need and deserve that information when asked to do something. This isn't an optional step a leader gets to decide whether to take or not. It is a requirement.

After you've asked those two questions and have given your audience the opportunity to ask any qualifying questions, then and only then can you hold them accountable for doing the task. Some leaders have a tendency to want to jump to the accountability component of their job description before going through all the steps in the communication model.

So some of you are thinking, "This sounds good, but I'm not in a position as a leader, therefore, this type of application doesn't apply to me." This actually is a simple example of how important it is to be able to anticipate a person's question and answer it before they verbalize it to you.

Okay, so you're not the CEO of Coca-Cola, a business owner, or even a manager. Are you maybe a parent? Do you maybe serve on a civic or church committee? Is there ever a time when you might need your spouse or friend to do something that they really don't want to do? Sure, there is. The same principle holds true in all these types of situations.

Now it is your turn. The next time you are in a position where you need to ask someone to do something, make sure you go through the five steps we just discussed and do your homework. It will pay off.

*I encourage you to get some practice now. Pick something that needs to be done and go through the steps. You might want to look backward rather than forward. You might think about an opportunity where you needed to get someone or a group to do something and it didn't quite go as you had hoped. Ask yourself, did you go through these steps? If you had to do it again, how would you have handled it differently by following the five-step communication tree model?*

# Personal Application

---

*I Believe in honest and clear communication*

I want to share three suggestions under this statement.

First, I've found when people are left in the dark, they don't think positive thoughts. Think about the last time you felt someone left you out of the loop on something. You didn't say to yourself, "Wow, this is great. It's pretty cool being the only one that doesn't know what's going on." Of course not. You were thoroughly upset and begin to think about all the possible reasons why you weren't included when this information was shared. You might have even started to think maybe this communication involves me or worse, is about me. You begin to think of all the negative reasons why you were left out.

Here's my rule of thumb when I have information to share. The first thing I ask myself is who could be affected by this information and get them in the "communication loop" early. The reason for this logic is this. If they are going to be affected by whatever information you are sharing, they will ultimately get in the loop down the road, and I've found when that happens, they are not a happy camper. They want to know why they didn't know earlier.

Second point is related to when you have someone come up to you and make a statement that just makes no sense. Immediately your mind goes to—what in the world were they thinking when they said that. That's the dumbest thing I've ever heard. There is a comedian by the name of Bill Engvall who has a routine that addresses this situation. He says, "Just give them a sign that says—I'm stupid!"

Well, that might make the listener feel better, but I don't believe it's going to generate great feelings on the behalf of the speaker. That's not the best first step in really trying to understand where this person is coming from.

My suggestion is when you find yourself in that situation and just want to slap some common sense into someone, change your game plan. Simply make this statement, "That's interesting. Help me understand why you feel that way." First, it's important that you actually mean what you are saying. Second, make sure you understand you aren't agreeing with them. You're just giving them the courtesy of acknowledging their statement by saying, "That's interesting."

Next comes the fun part. One of two things will happen, and both are good. As that person begins to explain what they meant, they may start to realize this doesn't make any sense and either say, "never mind" or change their message to something that hopefully both of you can understand. The second option is they go into great detail about the thought behind their statement and even though you might still think it is crazy, at least you know what their logic was in making the statement. Now if you want to get into a discussion on why you don't agree, at least you know where they are coming from and know what specifically to challenge in their statement.

The final point I want to make on clear communication relates to making sure you are clear on what someone just told you or asked you to do. One simple way to do this is to ask the speaker If it's okay to repeat back to them what you thought you heard them say or what they asked you to do. Tell them you want to make sure you heard them correctly. It actually shows the speaker you really want to make sure you got everything they wanted you to hear.

When you repeat back in your own words what you heard, one of two things will happen. One of the speaker says, "Yep, that's what

I said, or nope, I need to tell you again because you didn't get it the first time." Either way is a win for both parties.

*As you think about improving the effectiveness in your communication both as a speaker and as a listener, what are some things you can start doing on your end that will help you do that. Just focus on your responsibilities.*

## Personal Application

# Takeaways on Communication

# CHAPTER 7

# Attitude

A negative mind will never give you a positive life.
—Bruce Van Horn

*I Believe I'm not going to be judged by the situations and conditions I find myself in, but rather by how I respond to them.*

Here's another spoiler alert: You and I are going to be in and out of situations our entire life.

Some of these situations we create for ourselves through our actions, decisions, priorities, and reactions. We don't have anyone to blame but ourselves. We have to live with the situation we created and work our way through it.

There's a second origin of situations. That origin is the actions of others. Other people create circumstances through their actions, decisions, priorities, and reactions, and because of that, we find ourselves dealing with a situation we now have to handle.

Then there is one more source of situations. It is called life. We didn't create the situation. Someone else didn't create the situation. Life just happened. The COVID-19 pandemic is an example. Sure, some of the pandemic was created by the actions of others, but the virus was the "invisible enemy" everyone had to deal with.

I saw a quote from George Raveling that read, "Life doesn't happen to you. It happens for you." That is just another way of stating the message in this *I Believe* statement.

How many of you have had to deal with someone who held their own "pity party" every time something happened to them? I see a sea of hands going up. If that's not bad enough, they also send out invitations for others to come and join the party. These people will suck every ounce of energy out of those who accept their invitations. Tell them you have a previous engagement and just can't be with them.

You and I have complete control over how we deal with what life brings us. It is all within our control. It seems like today more people focus on whom they can place the blame instead of dealing with it. Our job is to take control of what we can control, and that is how we respond. We write that book; it is not coauthored by others unless we let it.

Dr. Mike Bechtle wrote a book titled, *People Can't Drive You Crazy If You Don't Give Them Keys*. I agree with Dr. Bechtle.

*What situation are you dealing with that you need to own, deal with, and move on? What past situations can you look back on and say I should have owned those and handled them differently rather than let them affect me the way they did?*

## Personal Application

*I Believe in not comparing myself to others and to other people's definitions of success.*

This statement became part of my *I Believe* list in two parts. On my original list, my statement read, "I Believe in not comparing myself to others." Let's talk about this part for a minute.

I don't know about you, but I have a full-time job being me. I do not have time to spend trying to be someone else. That said, we somehow figure out a way to make time, don't we? We've all tried to wishfully project ourselves into someone else's life. Don't beat yourself up if you fall into that category. Unfortunately, it's part of our human nature. We all grew up next door to the proverbial "Jones family."

However, here's what I found out when I became jealous of another person's life. I usually discovered as I began to examine their lives more deeply—all the "stuff" that they were actually dealing with that they never let anyone on the outside see. They had issues just as I did.

Ironically, I think it's safe to say there are probably other people that we may or may not know who are envious of our lives, and here we are wanting to be like someone else. We need to get off this jealous, envy-driven carousel and start appreciating who we are and how we have been blessed.

Back around 2006, I added the second part to my original statement, "and other people's definition of success."

If you went out, took a survey of everyday people, and asked them to share how they defined success. I think you'd get answers like this:

- Wealth
- Big house
- Lake or beach house
- Own my company
- Good health
- Nice car
- Member of country club
- Do what I want to do

- Retire early
- Have a great family
- Strong faith
- Influential friends
- Happiness

There is nothing wrong with any of the items on this list. Everyone gets a choice when it comes to what he or she wants out of life and how success is defined, but the problem becomes very painful when you haven't taken the time to define what success looks like for you and then end up trying to live your life up to somebody else's definition of success.

As an adult, have you ever thought:

- I don't have as nice a house as he/she does, so I must not be successful.
- I don't have as nice a car as they do, so I must not be successful.
- I don't make as much money as he/she does, so I must not be successful.
- I don't own my own business, so I must not be successful.
- I didn't retire at fifty, so I must not be successful.
- I don't take the type of vacations some people take, so I must not be successful.
- I don't have a lake house, so I must not be successful.
- I can't do the things for my children that they do, so I must not be successful.
- I don't have a college degree, so I must not be successful.

As a young person, have you ever thought:

- I'm not as popular as he/she, so I must not be successful.
- I'm not as good of an athlete as he/she, so I must not be successful.
- I don't have as good of grades as he/she, so I must not be successful.

- I didn't get into such and such college, so I must not be successful.
- I don't want to go to college. It's not for me. I must not be successful.

I could continue, but I think you get the point. We play the comparison game all the time because we do not take the time to really think about how we are going to define success as it relates to our life.

The truth is this. If you and I don't define what success looks like for us personally, we have no choice but to try to live up to someone else's definition of success. If we don't define what success looks like, how in the world would we try to chart our course to get there?

That truth hit me in 2006. Let me explain my story and how it affected me.

I did a poor job of personal planning when it came to vehicle purchases, and in 2002/2003, I needed to buy two vehicles. My wife and I decided we would by a small truck, and I'd use that primarily to go back and forth to work. The second vehicle would be a really nice car that would last us a long time. My wife would drive that car so we could keep the mileage down and extend the life of the car. I would use it when I needed it for business. We'd always had nice cars, but not a "really nice" car. Who am I kidding? I wanted a luxury car, and my wife went along with me on this.

Well, that's what we bought. A friend told me about a company that serviced Mercedes as well as searched for Mercedes for clients. That was the route we took, and we ended up purchasing a 2001 Mercedes E320 with only 31,000 miles on it. It was a sweet car, and by far the nicest car we'd ever had. We followed our plan and kept the mileage down, and the car lasted thirteen years. The car had approximately 260,000 miles on it before we decided to trade it in for another car.

However, that is not the story I want to share. About three years after we purchased the car, I came clean with myself. I didn't push to buy that Mercedes because it was a car that would last us a long time, even though it did. I pushed for it because it was a Mercedes! What is it that is associated with Mercedes's owners? Success!

This happened because I had never really defined what success looked like for me and I was trying to live up to other people's definition of success. That epiphany really changed the direction of my thinking and my priorities. I began to think, *What does success look like for me? How would I define it in my own words?*

Here is what I came up with. My definition of success is to be a positive influence in the lives of others. Boom! This became my new priority, what I work toward, and how I measure how I'm doing.

Once I realized what my true definition of success was, I told my wife, "We're going to drive this Mercedes until the wheels come off. But when that time comes, I'm going to go in the opposite direction of car purchases and get something very simple with no frills."

I wasn't going to tempt myself with another luxury car and slip back into that definition of success.

As I said, we drove that car for 260,000 miles, and then I told my wife I was going to go out and look at cars. She nodded and away I went, alone. The operative word is alone. My wife did not go with me. Not only did I look at cars, but I also traded in the Mercedes and purchased a 2015 Kia Optima that day.

I purchased the basic model, and when I say basic, I mean basic. To be more specific, it doesn't even have power seats. I'm not talking about heated seats. I'm talking about a button that can move the seat up and down, backward, and forward. It has a manual handle underneath the seat that you had to work to get the seat to move. Also, the car had no backup camera. So basically it doesn't have any real extras or what many people would consider standard features in today's car market, but it is a good-looking car and has a good safety record.

I had accomplished my mission.

Nevertheless, when I got home, I began to question my mission! My wife was not thrilled with my purchase. There is nothing wrong with a Kia, and she really wasn't ever a luxury car type person, but that was not the problem. She questioned the fact that in her mind, the car was "stripped." No extras. In fact, it turned out the passenger side seat couldn't even be adjusted manually for some reason. They had just made it that way. She is on the short side, and we had to put two cushions in her seat so she could sit at the safe and proper height.

Okay, maybe I went a little extreme on the "no extras" side of the purchase, but I still accomplished my goal of getting a car that was reliable and safe and not associated with luxury. The final chapter of this story concludes with my wife, in no uncertain terms, clearly informing me this will be the last car I purchase without her present. So be it.

*How do you define success?*

## Personal Application

*I Believe in learning from the past, but not dwelling on it.*

This statement will have an application that is more tangible as people age but can also apply to young people as well. All of us have a past. For some people, their past is larger than their future. For others, their past is a fairly recent part of their lives. In all cases, we have a past, a present, and a future and how we handle our past can definitely impact our present and our future.

A common message you hear from older people is to always learn from your experiences. That is good advice, and I believe in that as well. However, there is a distinction between learning from them and dwelling on them. Learning from experience means to analyze what you learned from an experience and be able to apply that knowledge when a similar situation arises in your future.

Knowledge alone is not powerful, but the acquisition of knowledge plus the application of that knowledge is when it becomes powerful. This is the proper use of knowledge or an experience learned.

Taking a bad experience and not learning from it can negatively affect your present and your future. One of the most devastating ways that can happen is by letting that bad experience continue to simmer in your mind. The result is that you continue to keep beating yourself up for the mistake you made. This is commonly referred to as dwelling on it. This type of action will continue to eat away at you and cause great harm.

Let me get totally transparent with you and share a personal experience. This is not a pleasant experience to share, but I do so regularly when I speak with young people or adults about my *I Believe* list. But every time I share it, it's painful to do so.

I was fortunate to be offered an assistant football coaching position at Georgia Tech the week after I graduated. This was a most unusual situation and one that I was blessed with. I always wanted to coach, and now I was going to get the opportunity to do it at the college level and at my alma mater.

Unfortunately, after three years of coaching football at Georgia Tech, our head coach decided to resign for personal reasons. Normally when a head coach leaves, the staff is also out of a job. That is what happened in this case. Welcome to the world of coaching college football. Now I had to find another job.

I was able to find my next opportunity at the University of Richmond in Virginia, where I coached for two years as an offensive coordinator. After my second year at Richmond, my mentor at Georgia Tech was named as the head football coach at the University of Virginia in Charlottesville, just down the road from Richmond. I had always told him if he became a head coach, I wanted to be considered to be part of his coaching staff. As it turned out, I was offered that opportunity, and after two years, left Richmond to join him. At that time in my life, I was married and had two young children.

Both schools were great opportunities for me and were promotions. It was also the first time I had been away from my parents and siblings. I was now truly on my own. I don't know what the life of a college coach is currently, but back then it was like the wild, wild west. There was a lot of travel for recruiting, late nights, and numerous opportunities to get into trouble if you were looking for it.

I made some poor choices and started hanging around with a few coaches who enjoyed that aspect of the coaching life. Nobody forced me to do it. Nobody twisted my arm. I wanted to see what that type of life was like because I sure hadn't experienced it prior to being married and starting a family, and definitely not after being married.

I believe there is an old saying that goes like this, "It's difficult to resist temptation when you go out of your way looking for it." Well, my partying coaching buddies and I went out of our way to find it! Not only did we find it, but we were also good at it and all that came with it.

During those four years, I lived that lifestyle every chance I could, and I was able to do so with no one in my family knowing about it. I was always able to cover up my tracks. I would feel guilty for lying, because that's what it was, and it would really bother me, but not enough to stop those types of decisions.

Those choices ended up affecting the quality of my coaching and my ability to look myself in the mirror. I knew what I was doing was wrong and hurtful because that wasn't the way I was raised. I'd become a Christian as a small boy but had certainly strayed from my Christian beliefs during that time. When that happens, guilt really sinks in. That is what was happening with me.

I went to my head coach, whom I mentioned previously had been my mentor at Georgia Tech, and told him I wanted to resign. He was aware of some of my activities, along with the other coaches who were involved. Let me be clear about one thing. Not all the coaches were "on this train," just some of us. He also knew I was a better coach than I was demonstrating. We talked at length, and I finally said I needed to get out of this environment and get back to living the way the real Jack Williams should live. So I resigned.

I returned to Atlanta to start a new career and started trying to get back to the life I wanted to live. Even after I started living the life I needed to live, the guilt kept growing and eating a deeper hole in me.

Fast-forward a few years, both of my children are now grown, and my son has a family of his own. There was a terrible tragedy in my son's life; he and his wife lost a child at birth. We were all just devastated about it, but in their grief, my son and daughter-in-law continued to praise God through and after that horrible event.

Their behavior really hit home to me. That is how I used to live. That's what living out your faith really looks like. However, that was not the faith my life was displaying. I immediately went to my pastor and said, "I now really understand what it means to have a personal relationship with Christ, instead of just religion." I told him the story of my son and daughter-in-law and shared my prior lifestyle issues. I said I wanted to rededicate my life to Christ and be rebaptized, which I did.

That was the first step. The guilt from the behavior I'd gotten away with without anyone in my family knowing was still weighing on me. It was like an anchor I was dragging through life. I knew I needed to do something but didn't know what that was.

Here is what I finally decided to do. I wrote individual letters to my son and daughter, and each of my five siblings. My parents were both deceased at the time, and I'll be honest, I don't know if I could have done this if they were both living. I'd like to think I would have been able to, but I'm not sure. My former wife and I had already worked through a lot of the issues surrounding our divorce, so I didn't send her a letter.

In my letters to my siblings, I explained in detail my activities in the past and how it wasn't the way I was raised. In the letter to my children, I also explained my activities in detail and how it wasn't the way I raised my children to be. I asked each of them for forgiveness.

I addressed the envelopes, put stamps on them, and placed them all on the edge of my desk in front of me. I was thinking, *When these go in the mail, my life is going to be changed forever!* I had no idea what kind of reaction I was going to get. The letters remained on my desk for three days before I had the courage to place them in the mail.

Waiting for my family to receive and read those letters was absolutely gut-wrenching. I just didn't know how they were going to respond. One by one, I got a call. My siblings were appreciative of me sharing what happened. In addition, they encouraged me that everybody makes mistakes, and that was a long time ago. Obviously, I was living a different life now. They said to move on from it. They could tell the toll my prior lifestyle had taken on me mentally, keeping this information inside and not confessing my mistakes. The healing process for my children was obviously slower, and rightfully so. It took some time, but we got through it, and I'm so grateful to both of them for working with me through that time.

I shared that long, very painful, and embarrassing experience in order to share this. As soon as I finished that act and got the responses, an unbelievable burden was lifted from my life. I can't express how different I felt. I could move forward without dragging that heavy anchor behind me.

This is why this *I Believe* statement is so important to me. I hope that through my painful confession, poor judgment, and secrecy, you can learn from my mistakes and can take and pursue the same solution I chose. Confess. Learn from it and move on with your life; try to be a positive influence in the lives of others.

*What baggage or anchors are you carrying around that are eating away at you? You know you need to confess and forgive yourself and move on with your life. There's only one person stopping you. Do it.*

# Personal Application

*I Believe I must successfully overcome my ego.*

You, I, and everyone else have an ego, and that's okay. An ego can serve a good purpose, but it can also be devastating to someone if it begins to be front and center in everything you do.

One of the best things that occurred in my life was being able to play QB for Georgia Tech and be named captain my senior year. It was a great experience, and it also provided some notoriety when I played, as well as afterward. For several years after I played, I would sometimes run into a person who remembered my name, and they would usually say nice things and want to talk football. I was always happy to do so, and it was fun reliving some of those good experiences. Oh, by the way, there were also some "stinker" games I didn't want to relive. You will get a sample of a couple of those shortly.

While playing and coaching, I received a three-year letterwinner ring at Tech. I also received a captain's ring for my senior year. As a player, we played in the Sun Bowl, and as a coach, our teams played in both the Liberty Bowl and the Peach Bowl. There were only about fourteen or fifteen bowls back then, not the forty or so that exist today.

Most of the Bowls back then gave watches as gifts to their players, and some of them were quite nice. Our Sun Bowl watch, not so much. I don't think it ever changed from El Paso time. However, when our Georgia Tech team played in the Liberty Bowl, Tech decided to design a unique Liberty Bowl ring and gave it to all of the players and coaches.

I really liked the Liberty Bowl ring because it was BIG and very noticeable. I would wear that ring every day. When I was talking with a business prospect or client, I would make sure they had every opportunity to get a view of that ring, hoping it would generate a question or a comment. I justified this in my mind by saying it was good for business, which sometimes it actually was. That was the same type of justification or logic that I applied to the purchase of the Mercedes. It was flawed. It was basically true but not the real reason I was doing it.

I finally realized that my ego was driving this behavior and it was not healthy. I decided that I needed to get my ego in check. One way to start that initiative would be to quit flashing that Liberty Bowl ring around. I figured the easiest way to make that happen was to remove it from my finger. I used my Georgia Tech education to come up with that brilliant solution.

Not only did I take off my Liberty Bowl ring and put it away, but I also put away my three-year letterwinner and captain's ring because I would occasionally wear those as well. Since I am being totally transparent, I have to admit when attending an important business appointment, I might have even worn two rings. What a jerk!

It has been probably fifteen years since I've worn any jewelry other than my wedding ring. That was the same time this statement joined my *I Believe* list.

One final comment on ego. I wear a Mickey Mouse watch. I know a lot of you don't wear watches anymore and use your phone for time. I still like to wear a watch. My choice of wearing a Mickey Mouse watch is not based on the fact that I'm a fan of Mickey and his gang. I wear it because it's difficult to walk around with a big ego when every time you look at your watch Mickey Mouse is staring back at you!

*Where are you on the ego meter? Is there anything you need to put away? Any behavior you need to change?*

## Personal Application

---

*I Believe in being responsible for the "Cans" in my life and giving to God the "Can'ts" and then getting out of the way.*

I have a list that I read each Wednesday morning in my devotion time. It lists the things that I feel are under my control that I need to be responsible for. Items on the list cover various areas of my life and business. After reviewing the list, I read over the items I cannot control and need to turn over to God. These are things that if they are going to happen, God is the one that's going to make them happen, and I've done all I can do.

Now let me say, a lot of thought went into what items go on which list. That was the hard part. I've spent a lot of my energy on things in which I had done everything I knew to do to make them happen yet they still weren't happening. That's when I realized, at this point, there was nothing more I could do, and if they were going to happen, they would have to be God's will and God's doing.

Now here's the tricky part. The last part of my *I Believe* statement says, "And getting out of the way."

Yep, you guessed it. I'm not doing that well on that part of the deal. Here's Jack's version of that statement.

"God, I'm turning this item over to You. I can't do anything more regarding it. I'm giving it to You, but it sure would be great if You could get it handled by Tuesday!"

Obviously, that's not giving it to God and letting Him truly handle it according to His will and His time. I am still working on this.

*If you were going to create a list like this, which I encourage you to do, what would be under each of the two headings? Would you be willing to truly let go of the items on the cannot list?*

## Personal Application

---

*I Believe in the concept that "more games are lost than won" in relationships and business.*

You're probably thinking about now that Jack is getting writer's block and just trying to come up with content. This *I Believe* statement just doesn't make sense. As Lee Corso says on the *College GameDay Show*, "Not so fast, my friend." Hang with me on this one.

This statement actually applies to multiple areas of your life. Let me explain by sharing the painful story that helped me learn this lesson. Earlier, I mentioned I played in a few "stinker" games. Well, here's the one that smelled the worst.

It was 1969, and I was the quarterback for Georgia Tech. We had an upcoming game on Saturday night against Notre Dame. Back then, there was only one prime time game on Saturday, and I think it started at 9:00 p.m. Notre Dame had one of the top teams in the nation that year, as they tended to do during that era. Ara Parseghian was their coach, and they had a guy named Joe Theismann as their quarterback. Theismann would later go on to have an illustrious professional career.

In order to properly set the stage for the events that occurred at nine that evening, we need to revisit an earlier game that year on October 4. That game was between Alabama and Mississippi, or as it is sometimes called Ole Miss. The two quarterbacks in that game were Scott Hunter for Alabama and Archie Manning for Ole Miss. This was an era of college football where teams mostly ran the football, as compared to today's game, where teams throw the ball all over the field.

I watched the entire game that day between Alabama and Ole Miss, and both quarterbacks had unbelievable games. They both threw for over three hundred yards, which was extremely uncommon at that time. In fact, Manning actually threw for over four hundred yards and ran for one hundred four yards; at that moment in time, no other quarterback in the history of college football had passed for four hundred and ran for one hundred. Alabama ended up nudging Ole Miss out 33–32 with a Scott Hunter TD pass with about four minutes remaining in the game.

Well, you might be thinking, that's some interesting trivia, but how does that relate to the Notre Dame vs. Georgia Tech game later that year? Here is how it relates.

During the afternoon leading up to the Notre Dame game, I kept thinking back to that historic matchup between Scott Hunter and Archie Manning. I became more and more excited and pumped about the upcoming matchup between Joe Theismann and Jack Williams.

This is where I need to share a little perspective on that thought. Joe Theismann was a nationally known player and a serious candidate for the Heisman Trophy, which goes to the top college football player. On the other hand, Jack Williams was a guy just lucky to be playing quarterback at the college level.

For more clarity, if I had to throw the ball fifty yards, I'd have to throw it, go pick it up and throw it again because I couldn't throw it fifty yards in the air with one throw. If they referred to speed and the name Jack Williams, it was usually preceded by the two words *lack thereof.* Thinking this was a duel between Joe Theismann and I was like saying there was a contest between a Mercedes and a Ford Pinto for Car of the Year, but that logic did not exist in my head that day.

To make a long story semi-short, I threw three interceptions in the first half and made two tackles as a quarterback. For you, non-football fans, neither of those stats are good. For you, football fans, you're probably thinking I've never heard of a quarterback making two tackles. Let me tell you, when you throw interceptions on national TV, the last thing you want to happen is for it to end up being a pick-six!

I was trying to make throws that I physically wasn't capable of making, and the result was disastrous for my team. However, because I was so pumped, and because I had these visions of another Manning/Hunter shootout, I did things I had not done before, nor would do afterward.

Late in the first half, I got sacked and suffered a mild concussion. The last thing Notre Dame wanted was for me to leave the game! Rumor has it that the guy who tackled me and knocked me out of the game lost his scholarship the next week. Perhaps just a rumor. I don't know, but I could understand their logic.

Why did I share that embarrassing experience? Because after that game, I realized a simple but very important fact. That fact is, in sports, more games are lost than won. What I mean by that is that one team normally ends up making more mistakes than the other team, and the team with the fewest mistakes usually wins.

Not only is it true in sports, but it's also true in business and in life. Think about relationships or marriages. When they don't work out, usually one of the parties "loses the game" because of what they did or didn't do. The same thing holds true in business. When a company signs up a new account and that account had been previously using that same service from a competitor, the new company didn't "win" that customer; the former company "lost" it because they failed to satisfy the customer and put them in play.

As painful as that national TV experience was, I learned a valuable lesson that night about how to "win." In fact, as a result of that night, I ended up focusing on what I could do best, which was to execute short to midrange passes. Oh, by the way, the coaches figured this out too. Because of that change, I ended my football career holding the career passing percentage record at Georgia Tech. Now that record has been broken many times since then, but it shows how results can change by simply understanding this simple truth.

I've also applied that same truth in business and have shared this concept with businesses when I conduct leadership workshops. Once they get over the idea that it's not a negative approach to business, they clearly see the value in applying it to their businesses.

*Since I have no way of knowing the demographics of who reads this book, I encourage you to take the time to think of some ways you can "lose the game" with your relationships, your business, your health, your academics, or your career. This truth applies to all of these. Get to work. You'll be glad you did.*

# Personal Application

*I Believe in dealing with reality.*

Perhaps I should rephrase that statement to read, "Facing and dealing with reality." I honestly believe this is a major issue in many people's lives. Let's start by defining reality. Reality, in simple terms, is the truth, the facts, or what's really happening, not what you hoped for or needed to happen.

What are some areas in which we may not be willing to face reality?

- Relationships
- Finances
- Time Management
- Health
- Habits
- Business
- Study habits and academics
- Job/career

Aldous Huxley once said, "Facts don't cease to be facts simply because we choose to ignore them."

If facing reality is such a prevalent issue today, and I think I'm right when I say it is, then why does it happen?

These are some examples of when I catch myself not wanting to face reality:

- Sometimes it's because I don't have another plan to replace the one that's not working.
- I've got a lot "invested" in whatever it is, and I don't want to lose that investment,
- It would be embarrassing to admit that I was wrong or that something wasn't working.
- My ego gets in the way.
- I am the boss and feel like I can't admit the idea was a bad one.
- I'm not willing to accept facts.
- If I admit something is not working, then that means I have to change, and I don't like change.

These are some of the mental gymnastics I've dealt with when facing a situation that wasn't working out the way I thought it would.

I hate to share another sports story, but you'll get a kick out of this one.

I was coaching football at the University of Virginia, and it was our second year trying to turn around a program that had a long history of being unsuccessful. We had suffered through a two-win first year and were lucky to get one of those victories.

Our second game was against the University of Texas. It was one of those games in which the weaker team scheduled a powerhouse team to play at their stadium in order to receive a big check. The weaker team justifies doing so to get the money to build their program and to get some exposure by playing a great team. That is the logic behind those kinds of games.

It was the second game of the season for Texas, and it was their homecoming. Who in the world holds homecoming the second game of the season? Well, if you play Virginia, you do. We played in so many homecoming games my two years at Virginia, we just started bringing our own float.

Back to the game. Texas won the National Championship that year, and we, at the University of Virginia, played our part in helping them do so. I knew we were in trouble during pregame. Check that; I knew we were in trouble when I saw Texas on our schedule.

Back then, most home team bands performed pregame shows, and that was the custom at Texas as well. As we were leaving the field after our pregame warm-up and started heading to our locker room, we ran into a problem. This was one of many that day. The Texas band was marching around the field to get to the end zone to start their pregame show. Unfortunately, as we were trying to get to our locker room, we had to encounter the Texas band which was directly in front of us. As a football coach, it's not encouraging to see your football team unable to get through an opposing team's band.

Texas had three All American players that year. One that had a lot of notoriety at the college level and later in the pros was a running back named Earl Campbell. He was a man playing with boys. In the first quarter of the game, Texas led 28–0, and Campbell had already rushed for 124 yards and had scored four touchdowns. Shortly after that, he had to leave the game with leg cramps and heat exhaustion. We ran him out of the game in the first quarter!

At half-time, the score was something like 48–0 or 42–0. In other words, a lot to nothing. I was the non-offensive coordinator that day. As we were leaving the field, the head coach said, "What do you think we ought to say to the team?"

I vividly remember responding by saying, "Coach, it's days like this you get paid to be a head coach. I'm not going to say anything to my guys. In fact, I'm not even going to go into the locker room."

He looked at me with this puzzled look and said, "What in the——are you talking about?"

I then shared my logic. I said, "Coach, it's 48–0. We are the University of Virginia. We have bright players, not necessarily good football players but bright guys. They know what has happened, and they know what's going to happen in the second half. This is the second game of the season. I'm not going to lose my credibility with my players by telling them all the things we can do differently in the second half because they know, you know, and I know, the final outcome is going to be determined by how many points Texas wants to score today. We, the University of Virginia football team, won't factor into the equation."

He cracked a small grin indicating he agreed.

As coaches, we agreed we were not going to go into the locker room at halftime. I have no idea what our team was thinking. They probably felt like we had already left and were waiting on the bus, and they probably wanted to join us.

The protocol before the beginning of the third quarter is for the referee to give both teams' coaches the five-minute warning until the second half kickoff so that both teams can get out on the field on time and get warmed up. This game "warning" was an appropriate term to use for us that day. Our head coach then asked all of the coaches to enter the locker room and gave one of the most appropriate and realistic half-time talks I have ever heard.

Looking down at his watch, he said, "Men," and then a short smile began to creep across his mouth, "I'm sorry, we've already cashed their check. We all have to go back out!" We lost that day 68–0.

Two years later, the University of Virginia had a winning season and beat the University of Georgia 31–0. Oh, by the way, it was Georgia's homecoming!

Facing reality can be painful. But if reality is, by definition, what's really happening—the facts, the truth—then we have to be willing to face it then react to what we see.

*In what area(s) of your life do you need to take an objective look and address a reality that for whatever reason, you haven't had the courage to face?*

## Personal Application

---

*I Believe it's my choice to choose whether to be a victim or a student when adversity strikes.*

You may be thinking the two key words in this statement are *victim* and *student*. You are correct that those are two very important words, but there's another key one. The operative word is *when*. The reason it is so important is because the first thing we have to understand is we *are* going to face adversity. It's not a matter of if, but when.

So if it's a fact we are going to face adversity, then it makes sense that we are to be prepared for it and to try to get a game plan in place for how we are going to respond when it comes. That makes sense, doesn't it?

I'll provide a simple example. I have a close friend, Mark Yates, who is on my Board of Directors at the IDEALS Foundation. He also teaches a class on the fundamentals of money management to our IDEALS Leadership Class. He doesn't talk about investing strategies, rather he shares the basic principles of how to deal with money. It's a great class and the students really enjoy it. He talks about planning for realities in your financial life. He likes to use an example regarding tires. He shares the fact that regardless of how good tires might be, everyone has to replace those tires after a certain amount of mileage. It's a fact. They are only going to last so long.

That said, what normally happens when we find out we have to replace our tires? We get in a panic. We start thinking, Oh no! I don't have the money to do that, or I wasn't prepared for that to happen. We then might put the tires on a credit card and build up our consumer debt burden.

However, there is another way to deal with a known expenditure in the future.

Mark tells the class, "If you know it's going to happen and about how long most tires last, then start putting small sums of money away each month to be prepared for that event."

Makes sense. I know that people don't have access to extra resources sometimes, but Mark's point is that many times if we make that commitment upfront, we can find ways to make that plan work. For instance, when the tires need replacing, we can just pull the money out of our savings, pay for the tires, and drive off. Then make sure you start back putting a little money aside each month to rebuild your savings account. That way, there is no need to get all upset, and no credit card debt. In this simple example of planning, we can be a student rather than reacting like a victim.

I mentioned earlier about the statement regarding how we cannot control all of the situations we find ourselves in, but we can control how we react to them. This is simply an extension of that statement. We have all been around people whose first reaction when something bad happens is to play the victim card.

They reactively say, "It isn't my fault. This isn't fair. Why did this happen to me?"

Sometimes they are right. It wasn't their fault, and maybe it isn't fair. Other times, this isn't the first time they've been in that situation, and clearly they didn't learn from their first experience. They didn't become a student the first time, and as a result, the victim appears at the scene of the accident over and over again.

There is always going to be a first time for everyone. It's those first times when something happens that we need to learn from and become a student, so when a second time comes around, we don't start yelling victim.

Think about the type of things that can happen during a normal life that most people would classify as adversity. Think about what could possibly be done in advance to be prepared and not be shocked when it happens. React with a clear head. Handle the situation and become a student from that experience. I realize sometimes you can't prepare, but you can control how you react.

And oh, by the way, start putting some money aside for those future tires, you are going to need it.

*What are some things you can start preparing for in the event they happen because some of them will?*

## Personal Application

# Takeaways on Attitude

# CHAPTER 8

# Family

Our most basic instinct is not survival but family.
— Dr. Paul Pearsall

*I Believe in family and that it is my responsibility to lead it.*

In an earlier section, I shared what a great family legacy my parents passed down to their children. We were truly blessed, and I have to admit since it's the only upbringing I know, I do have difficulty relating to others who have had challenging childhoods.

One of the things I don't have difficulty understanding is the fact that a family needs to be led. Personally, I believe that is the role of the man. The Bible tells us that.

Let me stop here and clear up one important fact. That does not mean a woman can't be a great leader of a family. We see that happening all over for two reasons. One, there are far too many single-parent households, and the leaders of the majority of those are phenomenal women. Second, in terms of marriages, the husband either isn't willing to step up, is uncomfortable assuming a leadership role, or doesn't possess the ability or desire to lead, and subsequently the wife takes that role.

In my family, my wife is by far smarter than I am, and she actually handles much of what most people would consider to be the "manly duties." She pays the bills. She is the mechanical mind of the two of us and is extremely organized. On the other hand, since my office has been in my home for a number of years, I assume a number of the household or domestic duties. I vacuum, wash clothes, clean bathrooms, and clean the dishes. You ought to see me decked out in my protective gear when I set out to clean the bathrooms. I'm a sight. In fact, one Christmas, my wife wanted a new drill, and I wanted a new vacuum. We were both thrilled when Santa delivered both of them to us.

As a couple, my wife is clearly capable of leading our family; however, that is the role I play. We work together, but she defers to me when we are not 100 percent in agreement on a matter. There are times when this occurs that my decisions don't turn out to be great or even right, but we haven't changed our model.

This is my second marriage. I have to admit I didn't do a good job leading in my first. I made mistakes and I wasn't the leader my wife and kids needed. That is a terrible regret in my life. I had to learn from that and not repeat the same mistakes. I have focused on being a better dad for my kids after that time and on being a better ex-husband than I was a husband to my former wife. Fortunately, my children turned out great, and my former wife and I have a very good relationship.

I shared this last embarrassing aspect of my life with you because some of you guys are where I was in my first marriage and think it's too late to change. It's not. Realize what you need to do to make things different, so you can be the leader your family needs.

Let me make one point clear. Leader does not mean dictator.

*Guys, what can you do starting right now to be the leader your wife and family need?*

*Ladies, what can you do to help encourage and support your husband to be the leader your family wants and needs?*

## Personal Application

---

*I Believe in praying for my wife and marriage* every *day*.

This is a must. Marriage is tough. The best marriages still have rough times, and we need to use every resource available to help us make and sustain strong, healthy marriages.

My *I Believe* list was created after my divorce. Had a number of things on this list been part of my life during my first marriage, maybe it would have had a different outcome. The divorce was on me; it was my fault.

I have a daily prayer routine and one of the most important parts of it is to pray for my marriage and my wife. You might be thinking, how do you pray for your spouse and marriage? What do you say?

Here are some of the things I pray for. Many of them are what you would think are obvious. Some are not:

I start by thanking God for how He has blessed us individually and as a couple. Then I lift up our children and their needs. Finally, I focus specifically on my wife and marriage.

- Health

- Safety
- Wisdom
- Discernment
- Unselfishness
- Clear communication
- Better listening skills (covered that earlier)
- Quality time together
- Serving my wife
- Self-discipline
- Thinking through issues and not getting emotional
- Being sensitive to her needs
- Making sound financial decisions
- Having a God-centered marriage

These are some of the things I think about on a regular basis when praying for my wife and marriage. Depending on what's going on in our lives or the lives of our children, obvious topics might get covered.

Also, I might add we have a short prayer each morning before each of us starts our days. Sometimes I lead the prayer, and other days my wife does.

One thing all married couples need to understand is marriage is a work in progress. I like to use the analogy of sign you sometimes see when there is work being done on a building that reads, "Pardon our dust, under construction."

*If you don't have this as a daily practice, I strongly suggest you start the process. Take this time to write down what you want to say initially until your thoughts, praises, and requests begin to flow more naturally.*

# Personal Application

---

*I Believe in not using the word "never" or "always" when having a disagreement with my wife.*

Stay with me on this one. Even strong marriages have those days when the two of you get into a lively discussion over some subject. If you are currently married, don't pretend this doesn't happen in your marriage. If you aren't currently married, hate to drop a spoiler alert on you, but you *will* have these types of interactions during your marriage. It is normal.

Frequently, in the course of many disagreements with your spouse, you, like my wife and I, might tend to throw in a few stronger terms to drive home your point. The two that my wife and I found out we were using too often were the words *never* and *always*.

Why these two words? It's simple; we used them for emphasis. My point could be far more powerful if it included either of these words. Saying you do this or that is not nearly as convincing as adding *never* and *always* to make your case.

I can be honest and tell you that when I inserted either of those words into my side of the argument, it turned my statement into a false one. My wife didn't *always* or *never* do whatever I was accusing her of doing. I was simply adding those words to make my position stronger in order to win the discussion.

We both agreed that was the case, and if we had to insert either of those words, then in reality, our point of view on that matter wasn't strong enough to stand on its own. The result of this self-examination and revelation was that we agreed to not use either word when having one of our lively discussions.

We also agreed that if either one of us lets one of those words slip into the conversation, the other had the right to raise their hand acknowledging that the other had violated the agreement. We both agreed that raising the hand to signal a "foul" was healthier in our marriage than raising the hand and doing something with it to get the other's attention!

*I hope if you are married that you will both sit down and address this* opportunity *to strengthen your marriage. It works. Map out your strategy now on how you will deal with it.*

## Personal Application

---

*I Believe I need a sound balance in my life—work, family, faith, fun, and rest.*

This will be a short narrative on this topic. This is another item on my personal list that tends to be accompanied by an asterisk. I am constantly trying to find that balance.

Having a fully operational office space in my home study is both a blessing and a curse. The blessing is I'm never late for work; the curse is I'm never truly away from work. My wife is constantly reminding me to step away from the computer, close up shop, and call it a day.

One of the things I'm really guilty of, unfortunately, is associated with the type of work I do and who I do it with. Many of my interactions are with students that are either currently involved in one of my leadership classes or are alumni. Since they are young people, they live in the world of texting. I often find myself sitting in the den with my wife watching TV, and all of sudden, I remember I need to send a text, or I get a text from a student. That irritates my wife, and rightly so, even though she knows it's part of my job. I need to confess here that all of these texts don't really have to be responded to immediately, but I usually do.

The same thing holds true when either of us has our phones nearby and we receive an email. Our first reaction is to stop what we are doing and see who sent what. And 99 percent of the time, it's not something that we need to address right at that moment. If it is important, the emails will keep coming until one of us responds. After several repeat emails, we realize this probably warrants some looking into, and we do.

One of my pet peeves is seeing a couple out on a date or having dinner, and they are sitting at the table looking at their phones. That's ridiculous! It used to be just young people, but now I see adults engaging in similar behavior. On several occasions, my wife has sensed I was about to leave our table and go say something to a couple on this matter, and luckily she wisely reeled me back in.

I really don't have a problem with the proper balance of faith in my life. As I said earlier, that's a priority for both my wife and me, and we react rather quickly if we see that part of our life being neglected.

Fun and rest are the other two aspects of this statement that require me to have an asterisk by it, which I'm working on. I'm not a person who is comfortable just sitting and doing nothing; it is just not in my nature. My daughter has inherited that same gene, and she sometimes struggles with balance as well. I hear about those people who talk about binge watching some TV show, and I've never been able to do that and really don't have a desire to do it.

I have a bad habit of thinking if I'm not doing something constructive, I'm getting behind and will regret it later. I love to play golf. I'm not good at it, but just good enough to want to keep playing, thinking I can get better. The golf industry is catered to people like me. Golf provides me both rest and relaxation and a nice break. I need to do more of it.

In addition, I do enjoy reading, and lately, I've been able to carve out more time to sit down and do that. In my earlier years, the majority of my reading was business-related or professional development, which obviously is beneficial but not necessarily relaxing. More recently, I spend my time reading a nice mystery or espionage book and let the main characters do all the work.

My wife and I have different interests when it relates to outside activities. You might recall she doesn't like to go to the gym! Now she loves to work in the yard and get exercise that way, and I enjoy yard work as well, but you can only do so much of that, and the weather becomes a factor there as well. My wife really isn't into playing some of the sports some couples enjoy like tennis or golf, and I'm not handy in DIY projects around the house like she is. As of late, we have been trying to find some activities we can do together with the goal of spending some quality time, combining fun and relaxation. This is still a work in progress project.

If this area is not a problem for you, I tip my hat to you. If you're like me, continue to work to create that healthy balance you know you need.

*What can you do right now to start moving the needle in that direction?*

## Personal Application

*I Believe when I'm with someone, I need to Be There.*

This statement could have been included in the "Relationships" category as well. However, I decided to include it here because even though I can be guilty of not doing this around anybody, I feel worse when I fail to do this when I'm with my wife.

There's nothing more frustrating than being with someone, knowing his or her mind is focused elsewhere. They are physically in front of you but nowhere close to "being there" with you. It doesn't make any difference what else is going on in a person's life, they owe it to the people they are with to give their full attention.

Today, so much attention is given to people being able to multi-task. I am not a fan of multitasking. I'll give you one simple example of why I feel that way.

I'm sure you've had a phone conversation with someone, and you can hear the keyboard working in the background. I'm not on the phone with that person for the purpose of them demonstrating they can multitask while talking with me. Sometimes I'll just quit talking and let them type away until they realize there is no longer a conversation taking place. When they ask why I stopped talking,

I simply would say, "I decided to let you finish typing whatever was more important to you than our conversation." Now that I have admitted how much that irritates me, I must state that I have to be careful from time to time that I'm not guilty of the same thing.

The other thing that can happen is that sometimes when you are speaking with someone on the phone or in person, you suddenly start thinking of something you have to do or have forgotten to do. That little voice in your mind begins to occupy more and more space in your thoughts, and now your attention has shifted from the person you are with to your thoughts about what you need to do later.

This is another one of the statements that from time to time has an asterisk by it on my list. I really have to make myself focus when those my thoughts wander and begin to attack my mind, causing me not to relate to a conversation with my wife or another person—and *attack* is the right word. The thoughts come at you, demanding to be given time.

It is important that when you are with someone to make sure you are totally there and give them your full attention. Be there and be present.

*Think about the situations in which you typically have a tendency to "not be there" when with another person. Make a note of these below and put yourself on guard to draw that protective shield in your mind to ward off those attacking thoughts. You might even ask those people you tend to do that with to let you know if they think you are drifting away from "being there."*

# Personal Application

# Takeaways on Family

❧

# CHAPTER 9

## Money

Money is a good servant, but a bad master.

—Frances Bacon

*I Believe in being debt-free.*

Most of us find out relatively early in life that debt is not our friend.

- It could be some money you borrowed from a friend that you are still struggling to pay back.
- It could be that college loan you took out so you could attend the college of your choice or be able to go to college.
- It could be that credit card balance that never seems to go down, even though you are making your monthly payments.
- It could be the car payment that is still with you when the car has no value.

We all have our story. I'm going to share a story about a member of the Williams's family other than me for a change. It involves my son, Brad. Brad was around sixteen or seventeen and wanted to go to Florida with a friend and his family for spring break. We allowed him to go. Well, the trip was an eventful one for Brad because while there, he met a girl. He hadn't previously been dating that much, and this young lady really got to him. When he returned, he informed us he needed to go back to Florida soon because this newfound love had invited him to her prom.

Initially, this was not looking like a trip we were going to sanction. First, there was the cost. Second, we weren't going to let him drive there alone. In order to discourage him, we told him he needed to look at various modes of transportation and the cost associated with each. We felt this would clearly snuff out the flame, but it didn't.

He came back and said he had found a reasonable price for a bus ticket. I almost laughed when I thought of him riding on a bus for probably twenty hours, stopping at every little town. I don't think he totally understood the routes that buses take on their trips. We informed him this was not going to be a luxurious mode of travel to get there, but he said he was prepared for that type of journey.

Then there was still the cost. We weren't floating in money, and we told him he would have to find work somewhere to be able to pay for the ticket and any additional expenses. We had paid for his first trip to Florida; however, we weren't going to pay for his second one.

The other pressing issue was that the prom was going to be held in just a few weeks, so finding work to get the kind of money he needed was going to really be difficult. This was when I realized how good my son was going to be in the future, regarding building relationships and marketing. He cornered the Joneses, a couple that my wife and I were friends with and asked if he could do yardwork for them to help pay for the ticket. He gave them the whole story about he really needed to get back and see this girl.

Here's where the plot thickens, and we address the subject of debt because he physically couldn't do enough yardwork to make the money he needed prior to the date he needed to leave, he asked them for an advance and promised he would work the balance off when he returned. The Joneses liked Brad and saw how serious he was about making this trip, so they agreed to the business proposition. It looked like the majority of the money that had to be earned was going to have to be completed by doing yardwork after his return.

Fast-forward to the trip. I started getting calls from my son about every third small town the bus stopped in. He said he didn't think the bus would ever get to his city. He also shared there were some people on the bus that "concerned" him. After multiple phone calls and two worried parents, he finally made it to his destination. He was only going to be there one day and then had to get back on a bus and make that long, arduous trek back home after the glow of the prom had worn off.

We never got the true details about the prom, but apparently it did not go quite the way he had anticipated. He was worn out after the long trip home, and he was now faced with a significant amount of yardwork ahead of him, for which he had already been paid. Several years later, the Joneses moved to Richmond, Virginia, and I'm not sure if my son doesn't still owe them several hours of yardwork on his open account.

Some debt is fine, as long as you have an asset to support it, and it represents an investment, such as a house. However, in today's society, that is not where the most dangerous debt resides. It resides in people living a lifestyle well beyond their means. The advertising world continues to tell us "we deserve such and such," and some of us have bought into the lie. Consumer debt is overwhelming the citizens of this country. Much of that is consumable debt, meaning people bought things that no longer exist or have value.

I worked with a man who I mentioned earlier named Mark Yates. We were officers in the same company. Each year when we got a bonus, he used it to pay down his house note. I used it for whatever was pressing at the time. It wasn't long before his house was paid off, and he owned it debt-free. I couldn't say the same about my house.

As we get older, we all have a lot of "do-overs" that we would like to happen. One of my biggest ones would be how I handled money and debt in particular. It took me a lot longer than I would like to admit to learn debt is not my friend.

Take a hard look at your existing debt and ask yourself, "Is it really justified?" Regardless, you have it now, and you have to figure out how to get rid of it in the most logical and appropriate way possible. One way is to create a systematic pay down schedule over and above what the normal schedule calls for. In other words, pay a little extra each month. If you get some extra money, use some or all of that to pay down debt.

This mindset goes against everything society is telling us. Society says, "Spend, spend, spend. You deserve this. You really need this." But in reality, no you don't.

*Make the commitment to start systematically reducing that debt and work toward that wonderful feeling of being debt-free. Here's a good place to list the debt you currently have and prioritize how you plan to reduce then eliminate it.*

## Personal Application

---

*I Believe money should be a tool, not a god.*

The Bible says the love of money is evil. It doesn't say money is evil. It all centers on how we view money and use it.

I'm like most everyone else; I would like to have more money than I have. I don't consider that a bad motive; however, it would be, if everything I did in life was focused on that objective. I hate to admit this, but if somehow I had been able to hit a home run financially at an early age, I'm convinced that it would have been a terrible thing to happen to me at that time in my life. You're probably thinking, he's crazy.

What I mean by that statement is that my perspective on money was not the proper perspective at that time, and I would have been a poor steward of it. If I were to be the recipient now of a tidy sum of money, I feel a lot more confident that I would handle that as a resource and a tool, rather than a god.

The whole concept behind creating my personal *I Believe* list was to set the right priorities in my life. One of those priorities center around one of the most desired objects in today's world, money. There's been a saying around for a long time, "If you want to see what's really important in a person's life, look at their checkbook and their calendar." Oh, so true!

I am not going to go into any more narratives on this subject other than to say there is nothing wrong with having money earned the right way. There is nothing wrong with becoming wealthy in today's measurements. The questions I want to leave with you are these: Are you going to control the money you've been blessed with, or is it going to control you? Are you going to use those resources as a tool for good, or are you going to worship money as a god?

Will you be a good steward of whatever financial resources you possess, or will you wonder what happened to them after you realize they are gone?

*As you think about those questions, what changes do you need to start making* right now *to become a better steward of your financial resources and to put them in the right perspective in your life?*

*Are you willing to avoid the temptations that will be there and demonstrate the discipline to do just that?*

## Personal Application

# Takeaways on Money

⚜

# CHAPTER 10

## Faith

All I have seen teaches me to trust the
Creator for all I have not seen.
—Ralph Waldo Emerson

Faith plays a very big part in my life. As I shared earlier, that was not always the case. I played church more than I truly understood what it meant to have a personal relationship with Christ.

This section will be shorter than some of the previous ones, not because it's less important, quite the contrary; it's because the statements that are contained in my list regarding faith are simple truths that don't require much narrative.

I want to go back to what I shared earlier in the book. This is *my* list of beliefs regarding my faith. You may be involved in another faith or no faith at all. I'm simply going to share what I believe and why. When you create your personal *I Believe* list, you can address this area in an appropriate way that suits your beliefs.

*I Believe God, His promises, and His plan of salvation.*

This actually is the only *I Believe* statement that is placed in any order on my personal list. It starts off my list. If I don't fully understand and live out this statement, the other statements on my list won't have near the impact in my life. There was an initial version of this statement that was on my list for many years before I revised it to read as it does above.

The original statement read, "I Believe in God, His promises, and His plan of salvation." Did you catch the difference between the two? It's the simple two-letter word *in*, but, boy, is it a *big* little word! By removing the word *in*, it totally changes the impact of that statement.

I personally find it very hard that people look around on any given day at the beauty, the splendor, the uniqueness of this world, and the people who live in it, and deny there is a God. I know there are those that take that stand. I just find it hard to comprehend. Think about all the complexities that make up our world—the human body and mind, plants, waters, nature, biology, planets, etc. To think there was not a master plan for all of that is hard for me to understand. That's what is meant by believing *in* God.

When I deleted the word *in*, it changed the entire meaning of my statement. I went from saying I believe there is a God to I believe God and everything He represents. I believe in His Word, His truth, and His way, along with the balance of the statement regarding promises and plan for salvation.

*In my opinion, I think the single most critical decision anyone should make in life is to answer the question—What do you believe about God? You just heard my answer, now what is yours?*

# Personal Application

---

*I Believe it must be about God and others before me. It's not all about me.*

A best-selling book, *Purpose Driven Life*, written by Rick Warren, opens up on the first page with the statement, "It's not about you." Talk about a bold opening to a book that you hope people will read. I wonder how many people saw that and said, "This book is not for me. I don't want to listen to that kind of nonsense. I like me, and I think highly of me. I dare him to say 'it's not about me.'" We will never know. However, the fact that it was a best-seller most likely indicates a significant number of readers continued on after the opening statement.

His statement really grabbed at me, which is exactly the reaction he wanted from his readers. Life is all about priorities. By having the first statement on my list be the previous statement we just discussed, I had to admit that he was right. It isn't all about me, although our world tries every way possible to convince us otherwise. Nevertheless, my *I Believe* statement takes it a step further. Not only am I not number one as the world would like me to believe, but I am also not even number two!

The word *others* is a catchall for the people in my life who need to come before me. That group would appear to be fairly obvious—family, friends, etc. However, "others" should also include those whom I don't consider friends or those I don't even know. Now I can't say I'm mature enough to stretch my statement to that group yet, but technically that's what it says. I'm still doing some "stretching exercises" to get me to that group, but I need to get there.

*Where do you rank in the order of priorities in your life? Who are some of the "others" that you need to look at differently?*

## Personal Application

*I Believe in being a good steward of God's blessings—money, things, time, talents, body, family, influence, and days.*

When we hear the word *stewardship*, we normally immediately fast forward to money. For example, some people believe you should be a good steward of your money, and that is a true statement. As I was writing this statement, I began to ask myself, what else have I been given the responsibility to steward or oversee? That is when I realized I had really shortchanged myself in understanding my stewardship job description.

I'm going to skip over the part about money, things, time, days, and family because we've touched on each of these in earlier statements. Let's focus on the remaining items in this statement—talents, body, and influence.

*Talents*

First, we all have to understand that each of us has a unique talent, but some may be more obvious than others. We also need to understand God didn't make any "junk." He gave each of us something we're really good at. Some obvious talents that come to mind are singing, sports, writing, speaking, investing, cooking, teaching, art, music, a technical or mechanical mind, etc. These are skills that we may have been born with, but each of those skills had to be developed for it to truly be a talent.

Just because you don't associate yourself with any of those talents does not mean you missed the talent train when it came to town. Let me plant a few seeds here with some questions:

- Is parenting a talent?
- Is being an encourager a talent?
- Is being a great friend a talent?
- Is being a great listener a talent?
- Is being a great spouse a talent?
- Is being a good communicator or teacher a talent?
- Is being a great neighbor a talent?
- Is being a mentor a talent?
- Is having a servant mindset a talent?
- Is being a good mediator a talent?

I could continue, but I hope you get where I'm going. I believe all of these are talents that we have the ability to develop, and each and every one of them is desperately needed.

*Body*

One of the biggest issues this country is currently facing—and it's just going to get worse—is the problem associated with the cost of healthcare. I believe this is occurring because we are not properly taking care of our bodies and our general health. Let me be clear on something. I'm not trying to be judgmental with this section. These are just facts. Look at what we eat. Look at how many people don't exercise.

I realize some people are more inclined to take care of themselves than are others. Self-discipline comes into play here, but it goes well beyond that trait. Exercising and taking care of myself is not a problem for me to make a priority. It started with my interest in sports, and if you played sports at the level I played, it wasn't an option whether to take care of yourself.

In the proverbial "good ole days," kids went outside and played. They didn't sit inside and use their thumbs to play video games and text. As a result, we were a healthier society because exercise was more of a normal part of our routine. I'm not just referring to gyms, running, etc. I'm simply talking about moving around a lot and not being sedentary.

There never has been a time in our society where there are more resources available for people to take care of themselves physically. There are no excuses. It's a choice and a matter of having the right priorities. Taking care of oneself goes beyond exercising. It involves eating the proper foods and the right amount of food in general. It means being aware of alcohol intake and definitely includes quality rest and sleep.

It's never too late to start doing a better job of making your current and long-term well-being a priority and reaping the benefits of doing so. When a person doesn't take this area of life seriously in terms of stewardship, you also are making yourself a potential liability to the people you love and love you—your family. You owe it to them to live the highest quality of life you can so you can be there for your family regardless of whether you are a spouse, parent, child, or grandparent. Remember it is not about you!

*Influence*

Most people don't think of being a good steward of their influence. Every one of us has a sphere of influence that our actions, behavior, beliefs, etc. either directly or indirectly affects. We mentioned this in an earlier section. We influence them by

- what we do,
- what we don't do,
- what we say,
- what we don't say,
- how we handle adversity,
- how we handle success,
- how we treat others,
- how we handle finances,
- how we handle responsibility,
- how we handle criticism,
- how we use our language,
- what the priorities are in our life,
- how we demonstrate that we are trustworthy, and
- how we demonstrate integrity 24/7/365.

That's just a few of the ways we can influence others. There are so many ways we can be an influence, either positive or negative, in the lives of others. You *will* be either positive or negative; you will never be neutral.

*Think through the list above. How are you doing in these areas? What kind of influence are you having on those in your sphere in these areas?*

*What do you need to start doing, stop doing, or continue doing to be a good steward in all the different areas of your life?*

# Personal Application

---

*I Believe if I can trust God for my eternity, I can surely trust Him for my daily activities.*

I sometimes catch myself forgetting this very simple truth. Sometimes I get worked up over something that is going on in my life or something I have to prepare for, and I feel overwhelmed and all stressed out. When I come to the realization that I've forgotten the truth in this *I Believe* statement, I sometimes just start laughing.

I've already said earlier I believe God, His Promises, and His plan of salvation. That belief is based totally on faith. I cannot earn that salvation. It's given to me as a result of my confessed faith through the grace of God. This faith is a real obstacle for many people. How can someone believe that there is life after death and eternal fellowship with God? That's a big leap of faith for sure. Yes, sir, it is. However, that's what God asks us to do, and I'm firm in that faith.

When I think about my willingness to make that kind of faith commitment to a God that can do all that He says He can do, including provide eternal life, how in the world can I think He can't handle this little thing I'm dealing with right now on earth? Think through that logic for a minute. It just doesn't add up, does it?

*What are you struggling with right now that is causing anxiety and concern? Do you think God is not aware of what is going on? Have you turned it over to him? Remember to focus on the items on your "can list" and give God the things that only He can handle that are on the "God only can" list.*

## Personal Application

---

*I Believe when I align my priorities with God, He will show up in dramatic ways.*

Have you ever heard of Garth Brooks's song that talks about thanking God for unanswered prayers? It's a great song with a great message.

I don't know about you, but I don't have time to get into details about the prayers, wishes, and desires I had that I thank God He never gave to me. He didn't because they weren't aligned with God's plan for my life. It wasn't the right time; I wasn't ready to handle them. Whatever the reason, it would have been a disaster if I had received what I had asked for.

We have repeatedly referenced the importance of having the right priorities in our lives. I found that it all boils down to this.

When my priorities are right, not selfish, not emotional, not knee jerk in nature, not shortsighted, and most importantly, not in conflict with God's Word, God has an amazing habit of showing up in dramatic ways and doing amazing things in my life. Now when I say amazing, I'm not talking about financial windfalls, hair on the top of my head (in my case), or things I really do not need. When I align my priorities with God's priorities, things happen. I'll readily admit that this is still a work in progress because I have the same human temptations, weaknesses, desires, and thoughts as anyone else. In addition, I have to be constantly on guard with what my true priorities are at any given time, and sometimes I fail. The difference is I know I failed and why and what has to change to get back on track.

Remember the old joke about the old couple driving down the road and the wife sitting on the passenger side next to the window starting to reminisce about the good old days?

The wife says, "Remember when we drove, we use to snuggle next to each other in the car. Couldn't slip a sheet of paper between us."

The old man looks at his wife and says, "I ain't moved!"

Well, when we don't get what we asked for, God's priorities haven't moved. Ours have.

*What do you need to do to start reevaluating your priorities so that they are aligned with what God wants for you?*

# Personal Application

---

*I Believe God is a sovereign God who is in control of everything.*

This is a tough one for a lot of people to grab hold of, and it wasn't on my original *I Believe* list either. This statement comes up usually when there is tragedy in our lives or craziness in our world. I get it. I clearly understand that questioning.

However, the Bible clearly states that God's ways are not our ways, and God's thoughts are not our thoughts. If we totally understand who He is and what His plan is for the world and our individual lives, then He wouldn't be God, would He?

It comes right back to the question—do we believe God and His Word? I do, and as I have said before, this is *my* list.

*What's keeping you from accepting this truth?*

# Personal Application

132

# Takeaways on Faith

# CLOSING THOUGHTS

Thank you for allowing me to be transparent in sharing my thoughts. Again, I want to emphasize the items on my list are based on *my* beliefs. I'm not writing this book to convince you to believe everything I believe. You have to make your own decisions regarding the priorities, values, beliefs, and truths you believe in. These decisions will ultimately shape who you are, what you become, and the kind of quality and balance your life will have. What I am trying to do in this book is to get you to understand the impact that having a personal *I Believe* list can have on your life. Hey, we're only talking about the quality of the rest of your life here!

Remember I said earlier in the book, "We all make decisions, and ultimately our decisions make us."

My goal for writing this book is to encourage you to make today *decision day*. The day you commit to start putting down in writing what you believe and then use that list as a reminder, an encourager, and a daily accountability partner. Not only to put these beliefs in writing but also

- to commit to letting them guide you to be the person you want to be,
- to be a positive impact on the lives of others,
- to be a positive role model to those in your sphere of influence,
- to be the best *you* that you can be, and
- to have your life be a mirror reflection of the statements on your list.

Remember, this will be a work in progress. Don't get discouraged if you start having a lot of asterisks on your list. That means you are actually being totally honest with yourself, and that's a good thing.

This exercise and this *I Believe* list have played a crucial role in shaping my life and what my life is going to represent between the "born date" and "died date" on my tombstone. I so wish I would have started this process at a younger age. Some of you fall in that category right now, and now is the time to make this life-changing decision. Some of you are adults, and you are still in your prime and have a broad sphere of influence that needs you to be a positive influence in their lives. Some of you are in your senior years. It's never too late to start doing what's right. Some of the most influential people in the history of our country "made their mark" through significant contributions in their senior years. Why not you?

Drop me a note and let me know how you are doing with your list. I look forward to hearing from you!

jackw@idealsleadership.org

God Bless!

⚜

# REFERENCES


"If you don't know where you're going, any road will get you there" (Lewis Carroll, *Alice's Adventures in Wonderland* 1865).

"The purpose of life is a life of purpose" (Robert Byrne).

"The privilege of a lifetime is being who you are" (Joseph Campbell, *A Joseph Campbell Companion: Reflections on the Art of Living* 1995).

"If you don't stand for something, you'll fall for anything" (Alexander Hamilton).

"There are three constants in life…change, choice, and principle" (Stephen Covey, *Principle-Centered Leadership* 1992).

"Treasure your relationships, not your possessions" (Anthony J. D'Angelo, *The College Blue Book: A Few Thoughts, Reflections and Reminders on How to Get the Most Out of College and Life* 1995).

"When wealth is lost, nothing is lost; when health is lost, something is lost; when character is lost, all is lost!" (Anonymous).

"A negative mind will never give you a positive life" (Bruce Van Horn. *Worry No More!: 4 Steps to Stop Worrying and Start Living* 2015).

"Knowledge is not powerful, but the acquisition of knowledge plus the application of knowledge is powerful" (Jack Williams, IDEALS Leadership School 2014).

"It's difficult to resist temptation, when you go out of your way to look for it" (Jack Williams IDEALS Leadership School 2010).

"Facts don't cease to be facts simply because we choose to ignore them" (Aldous Huxley, *Complete Essays 2, 1926–'29* 2000).

"Our most basic instinct is not survival, but for family" (Paul Pearsall, *The Heart's Code: Tapping the Wisdom and Power of Our Heart Energy* 1999).

"Money is a good servant, but a bad master" (Francis Bacon, *The Essays* 1597).

"If you want to see what's really important in a person's life, look at their checkbook and their calendar" (Anonymous).

"All I have seen teaches me to trust the Creator for all I have not seen" (Ralph Waldo Emerson, *Self-Reliance and Other Essays* 1844).

"It's not about you" (Rick Warren, *A Purpose Driven Life* 2002).

# RESOURCES

Jack Williams's I Believe List (Tenth Edition)

- I Believe God, His promises, and His plan of salvation.
- I Believe in family, and that it's my responsibility to lead it.
- I Believe in establishing a good name and preserving it through my actions.
- I Believe my integrity and character must not be compromised.
- I Believe I'm not going to be judged by the situations and conditions I find myself in but rather how I respond to them.
- I Believe in being faithful to my wife.
- I Believe in forgiveness—for me, by me of others, and forgiving myself.
- I Believe in being a positive role model.
- I Believe in complimenting people when they do a good job.
- I Believe in not comparing myself to others and other people's definition of success.
- I Believe in honest and clear communication (transparency).
- I Believe in taking care of myself physically, spiritually, and emotionally.
- I Believe in always continuing to learn and improve.
- I Believe I need a sound balance in my life—work, family, faith, fun, and rest.
- I Believe in being organized and prepared in whatever I do.
- I Believe in discipline and the value it brings to my life.

- I Believe we all make decisions, and ultimately our decisions will make us.
- I Believe in being a good listener, showing respect to the other person talking.
- I Believe in being a good friend and being there when needed; it's a privilege and a responsibility.
- I Believe in identifying the true "drivers" to a successful and meaningful life.
- I Believe it must be about God and others before me. It's not about me.
- I Believe in being a good steward with God's blessings—money, things, time, talents, body, family, influence, and days.
- I Believe in being aware of the various habits in my life, both good and bad.
- I Believe in telling people I love them.
- I Believe in doing the "next right thing."
- I Believe in personal accountability.
- I Believe in tithing.
- I Believe there are always going to be consequences to our decisions—good or bad.
- I Believe in the power of prayer and claiming God's promises.
- I Believe I will ultimately be defined by my impact on the kingdom and the "forever" in the lives of people.
- I Believe I can do and handle all things through Christ who strengthens me.
- I Believe I must place my trust and faith in God, not in my own abilities.
- I Believe in telling people I believe in them.
- I Believe in growing spiritually and spending time in God's word.
- I Believe in learning from the past, but not dwelling on it.
- I Believe my "life signature" will be determined by my *I Believe* list, how I define success, and the quality of my decisions.

- I Believe I need to overlook the "small stuff" in relationships.
- I Believe in treating people with dignity and respect and not being judgmental.
- I Believe I must successfully manage my ego.
- I Believe God is still in the miracle business.
- I Believe God is a sovereign God and in control of everything.
- I Believe I need to be flexible and willing to change as needed.
- I Believe in understanding the difference in teaching and telling.
- I Believe in being responsible for the "cans" in my life and giving God the "can'ts" and getting out of the way.
- I Believe I need to spend more time investing in others. Life is about relationships.
- I Believe in showing my wife the attention I gave her when we were dating.
- I Believe in not using the words *never* or *always* when having a disagreement with my wife.
- I Believe if I can trust God for my eternity, I can surely trust him for my daily activities.
- I Believe in the concept that "more games are lost than won" in relationships and business.
- I Believe in being debt free.
- I Believe the quality of my personal relationship with Christ is my responsibility.
- I Believe when I align my priorities with God, He will show up in dramatic ways.
- I Believe I need to seek first His kingdom and His righteousness and let Him take care of the rest.
- I Believe in voting and working to help our nation return to our biblical and constitutional foundations.
- I Believe money should be a tool, not a god.
- I Believe in finishing strong; family, faith, work, finances, influence, giving, and health.
- I Believe in the sanctity of life.

- I Believe in dealing with reality.
- I Believe when I'm with someone, I need to Be There.
- I Believe in doing what I say I'm going to do or what I know I should do.
- I Believe in being "all in" in the key areas of my life.
- I Believe through IDEALS, I can be a positive impact in helping young people become positive role models and influential leaders.
- I Believe I have the same amount of time as everyone else; it's my responsibility to plan and prioritize it.
- I Believe in seeking wise counsel on important issues. I don't have all the answers.
- I Believe I have total control of my attitude daily.
- I Believe in being a good "steward" of each day. It's a blessing from the Lord.
- I Believe I'm always just one bad decision away from doing irreversible damage to myself and others.
- I Believe it's my choice to choose whether to be a "victim" or a "student" when adversity strikes.
- I Believe in praying for my wife and marriage *every* day.
- I Believe in patience, persistence, and perseverance.

❧

# "I BELIEVE" CATEGORY EXAMPLES

Faith

Family

Career

Finances

Relationships

Dating/Marriage

Health

Character

Lifestyle

Personal Development

Leadership

Helping Others

Tithing

Values

Athletics (short-term issue)

Decision-Making

Dependability

Time Management

Priorities

Communication

Academics

Giving

Role Model

Establishing a Good Name

How You Treat People

Respect

Trustworthy

Accountability

Goal Setting

Discipline

Listening

Balance in Your Life

Political Principles

Responsibility

# DECISION-MAKING GUIDE

*Remember*
We all make decisions and ultimately our decisions will make us.
There are consequences for every decision we make—good or bad.
You will be the product of the decisions you make *today*.


*Decision-Making Process—Questions*
Why do I want to do this?
What are the facts? Do I have enough facts, or do I need more?
    Where can I go to get more facts?
Do I have enough information to make this decision?
What do I think are my various options?
What happens if I decide to do nothing?
What are the benefits and potential consequences?
What would be my backup plan if this turns out to be a bad decision?
What "I Believe" statements relate to this issue?
Who might be affected by this decision and how?
How much time do I have to make this decision?
Am I thinking clearly? Have I really thought this through?
Is this what *I* really want to do?
Am I rushing this decision?
Am I being impulsive?
What are the chances that I could regret this in the future?
Is anyone trying to influence my decision?
What do I feel are their motives for doing so? Are they properly aware
    of the facts?
How might this decision affect my "brand"?
Is this decision in alignment with my goals in any way?
What is stopping me from making this decision?

Do I have peace about this decision?
Who can I go to for advice?
*Finally, if my decision was made public to everyone, how would I feel?*

# ACKNOWLEDGMENTS

Anytime when an author writes a book, it is a team effort. When it is an author's first book, it is even more so. I want to thank all of the people that I had the privilege to work with and learn from during my business career. The names are too many to share here, but you are a special group of men and women who had a great influence in my life.

The students who go through my IDEALS Leadership School are the young people who allow me to pilot much of my content and ideas in those classes. I'm grateful for them working with me all these years and for the impact each of them has had on my life.

Thanks to my wife, Lisa, for putting up with me when I often dart from the den to my home office to take a call or to work on an idea at night. Thank goodness, she likes TV!

I want to thank Danny Rowe, Ron Riley, Jimmy Stokes, Stan Beavers, Brad Williams, Art Hall, John Vaughn, and David Williams for giving their time to read a *really* rough first draft of this book and for sharing their thoughts and ideas. Their input was extremely helpful.

My daughter, Jennifer Baker, was kind enough to put her English teaching literary skills in play to do the initial editing for the book. Could not have done it without her efforts. She had the tough job!

This book would have never made it to press had not Madisen Mayfield paved the way for me. Madisen was about one month ahead of me in where she was in writing her first book. She gladly walked me through the final stages of getting my book published, and actually she handled many of those duties personally.

Finally, I want to express my appreciation to each of the wonderful people who invested their time to read my book and share their comments represented in the front of the book. A big thank you goes out to each of you.

# ABOUT THE AUTHOR

Jack Williams is a native of Decatur, Georgia. He received a bachelor of science degree in Behavioral Management from Georgia Tech. As a quarterback for the Georgia Tech football team, he was a three-year letterwinner and was named team captain his senior year. After graduating from Tech, Jack became an assistant college football coach for seven years. He coached at Georgia Tech, the University of Richmond, and the University of Virginia.

He then began a thirty-year career in business, holding leadership positions as COO of a regional service company, as senior vice president/general manager of a $220-million division of a Fortune 500 company, and as president of a contract staffing firm.

While working in the corporate world, Jack formed the IDEALS Foundation in 1993. IDEALS is a nonprofit educational foundation designed to help young people develop their leadership and life skills. The IDEALS Leadership School, which also began in 1993, is still working with high school students today. Also, most recently, he was asked by the Georgia Department of Education to create two life/soft-skills video programs for Georgia students. He is now expanding those programs nationally.

In addition, Jack's business consulting firm, the Timbridge Group, conducts leadership workshops with companies across the country.

Jack and his wife Lisa reside in Lawrenceville, Georgia, and have four adult children and seven grandchildren.

www.ingramcontent.com/pod-product-compliance
Lightning Source LLC
Chambersburg PA
CBHW021203130726

47988CB00002B/489